Wilhelm Kücker
Deutsche Bank Essen

Wilhelm Kücker
Deutsche Bank Essen
herausgegeben von
edited by
Ingeborg Flagge

Wasmuth

Herausgeberin und Architekt danken der
DEBEKO Immobilien GmbH
& Grundbesitz OHG
für die Förderung dieser Werkmonographie.
The editor and the architect wish to thank the
DEBEKO Immobilien GmbH
& Grundbesitz OHG
for their support of this publication

Wilhelm Kücker
Deutsche Bank Essen
herausgegeben von
edited by
Ingeborg Flagge, Bonn

Übersetzungen
Translations
David Bean, Berlin

Fotografie
Photography
Deimel + Wittmar, Essen

Gestaltung
Graphic Design
Joachim Mildner, Köln

© Ernst Wasmuth Verlag, Tübingen · Berlin

Printed in Europe/Germany 1998

Die Deutsche Bibliothek – CIP-Einheitsaufnahme
Kücker, Wilhelm:
Deutsche Bank Essen
Hrsg. von Ingeborg Flagge
-Tübingen: Wasmuth, 1998.
ISBN 3-8030-0177-3

Inhalt
Contents

7   Vorwort

9   Wenn Banken bauen
    Ingeborg Flagge

15 Renovierung und Neubau der Deutschen Bank Essen, 1993–1997
    Winfried Wang

67 Preface

69 When Banks Build
    by Ingeborg Flagge

75 Renovation and New Construction of the Deutsche Bank
    Building in Essen, 1993–1997
    by Wilfried Wang

80 Projektdaten

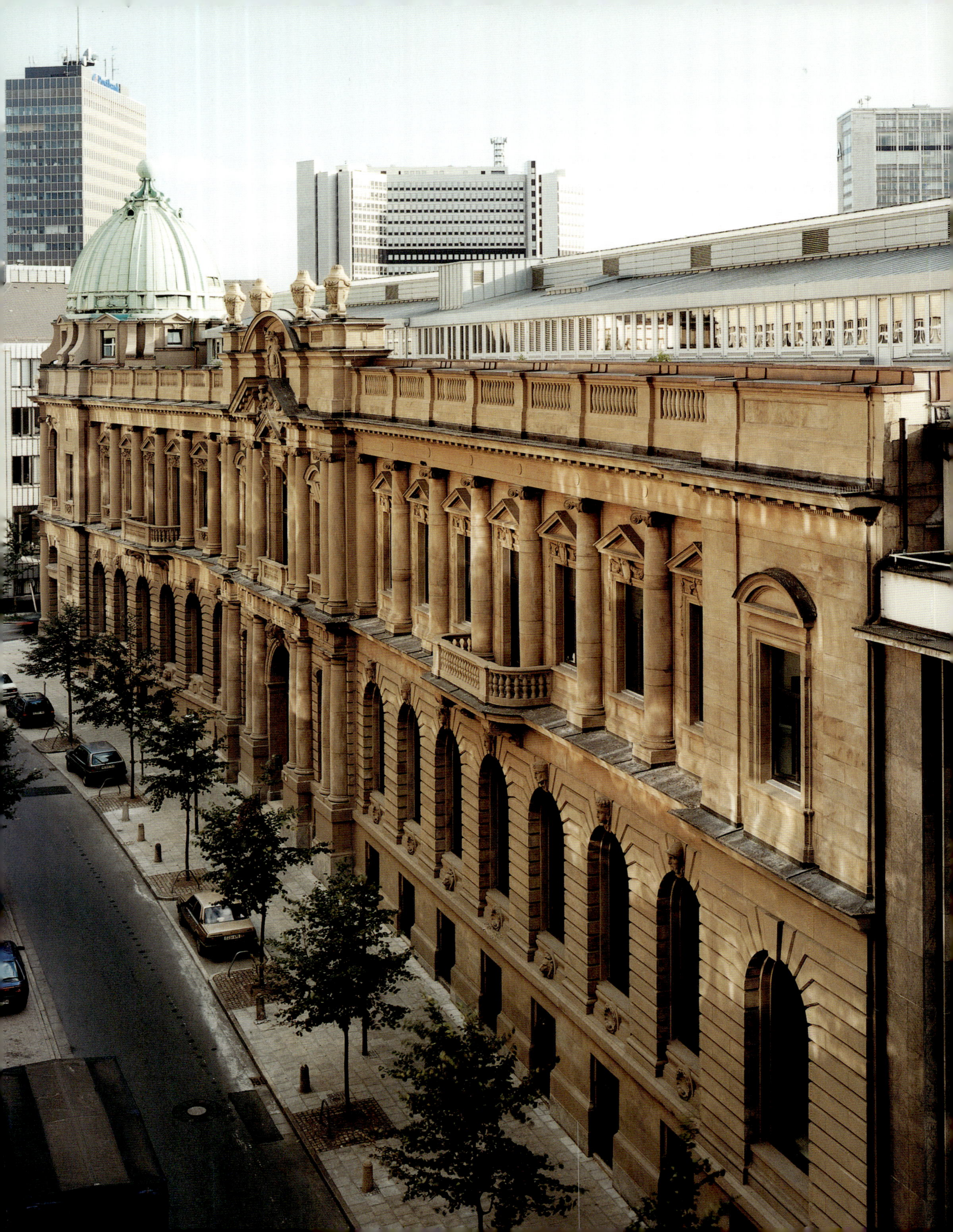

Eine Bank ist eine Bank ist eine Bank ...

... könnte man in nüchterner Abänderung des poetischen Satzes von Gertrude Stein „Eine Rose ist eine Rose ist eine Rose" [„a rose is a rose is a rose"] formulieren. Eine Bank ist eine Institution, die – im weitesten Sinne des Wortes – mit Geld handelt und daran verdienen will und muß. Gleichzeitig ist die Bank der gebaute Ort, wo genau dieser Handel stattfindet. Daran hat der Computer wenig geändert.

Doch während sich früher die Funktion der Bank weitgehend auf das Geschäftemachen konzentrierte, ist dies heute längst nicht mehr der Fall. Banken sind schon lange nicht mehr reine Wirtschaftsunternehmen. Sie sind – besonders im Fall der Deutschen Bank – auch Förderer und Sammler der Künste. Sie verstehen sich als Sponsoren im Kunstbereich – und dies auf ganz unterschiedlichen Gebieten.

Das ist auch der Grund dafür, daß sich die Deutsche Bank zu anspruchs- und qualitätvoller Architektur bekennt, zu Baukunst; egal ob es sich dabei um altes historisches oder um neues zeitgenössisches Bauen handelt. Die Zeiten, in denen Banken selbstherrlich die Architektur für sich bauten, die ihnen zusagte, und sich dabei um die öffentliche Meinung nicht scherten, sind lange vorbei. Hier haben die Banken aus den Protesten der sechziger und siebziger Jahre gelernt.

Bankbauten sind selbstverständlich, wie dies schon früher der Fall war, eine Frage des Images. Aber die Banken betreiben die Form gebauter Selbstdarstellung heute eher in Zusammenarbeit mit der Gesellschaft, nicht gegen sie. Bankbauten sind auch längst nicht mehr wie früher konservative Bauten, Tempel des Geldes, womöglich noch in historischem Gewand.

Wo es sich wie bei dem Bau der Deutschen Bank in Essen um aktiven Denkmalschutz in der Erneuerung und Ergänzung eines markanten Altbaues handelt, stellt sich die Bank dieser Verpflichtung mit dem Mut zur innovativen Gestaltung.

Der beste Denkmalschutz ist der, der die Sprache eines Altbaus aufnimmt und sensibel und behutsam in einen zeitgemäßen Bau umsetzt. Genau dieses Kunststück – Baukunst – hat Wilhelm Kücker in Essen bewirkt.

Ingeborg Flagge

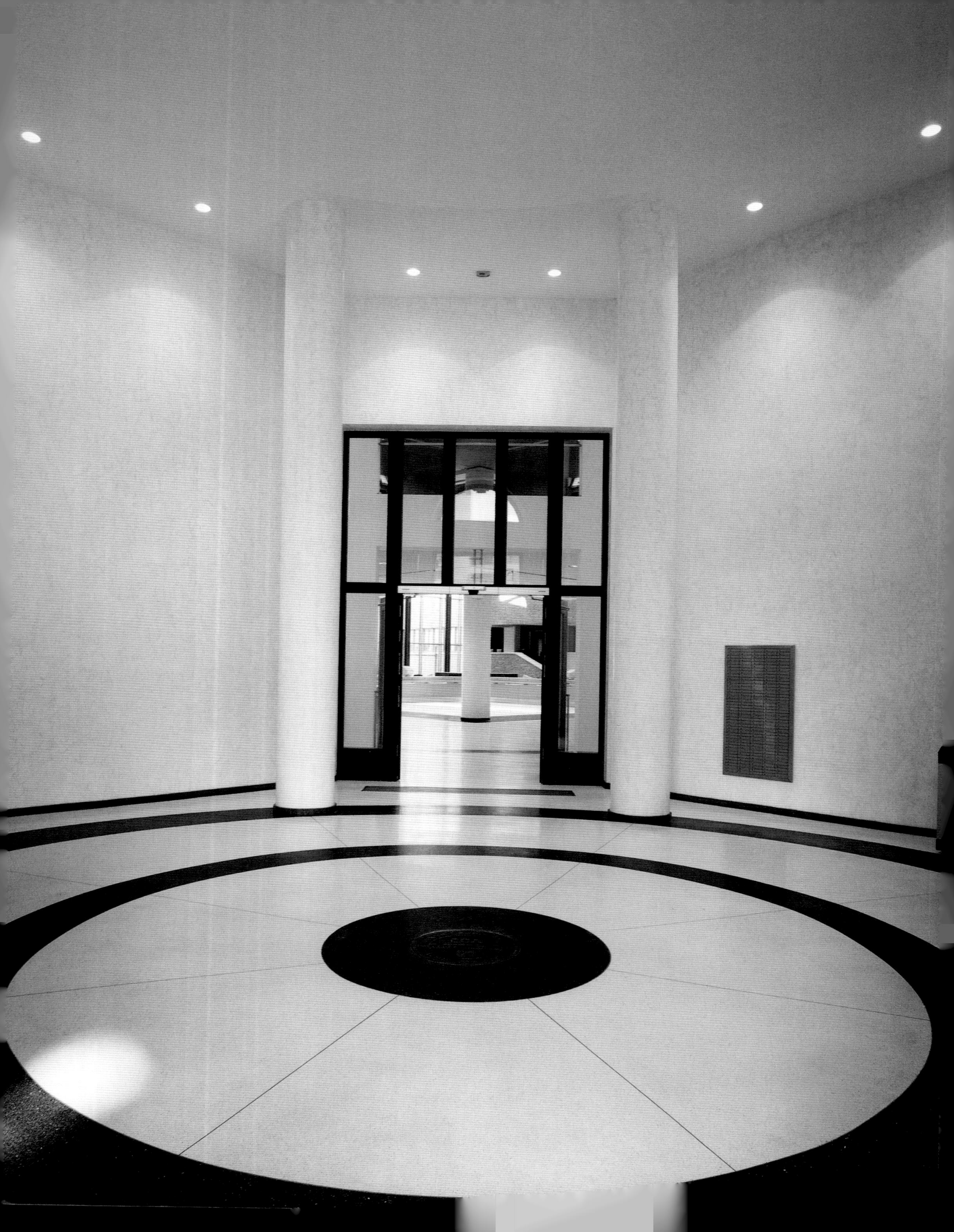

Wenn Banken bauen

Das Geschäft mit dem Geld fand erst verhältnismäßig spät zu einem Bautyp; demzufolge ist, gemessen am Wohnungs- und Tempelbau, die Geschichte von Bankgebäuden relativ jung.

In Ägypten, wo noch ein bargeldloser Zahlungsverkehr herrschte, unterhielten Kaufleute und Grundbesitzer bei Staatsspeichern Konten mit Last- und Gutschriften. In Griechenland dürften zunächst Priester bankierähnliche Funktionen ausgeübt haben; sie nahmen Einlagen zur Aufbewahrung im Tempel entgegen und gewährten Darlehen gegen konkretes Entgelt. Als sich dann das Münzwesen durchzusetzen begann, entstand in Griechenland ein neuer Beruf: jener der Trapeziten. Der Name leitet sich von „trapeza" = „Tisch" ab, dem Untersatz, auf dem die neuen Geldherren Münzen prüften und wechselten. In Rom gab es bereits den anerkannten Berufsstand der „argentarii" oder „mensarii", eine Art privater Bankierszunft, die neben den staatlichen und priesterlichen Geldhändlern lukrative Geschäfte betrieb.

Spezielle Bauten für dergleichen Geschäfte gab es noch nicht. Geld, Gold und Wertsachen des Staates lagerten in gutbewachten Schatzhäusern und -kammern. Der einzelne mag wertvollen Besitz in einer Truhe aufbewahrt oder in seinem Haus versteckt haben. Der Handel und Austausch dürfte weitgehend unter freiem Himmel stattgefunden haben; die Geschichte des Bankenbaus ist denn auch eine vom offenen Markttisch bis zum heutigen Hochhaus.

Der Ursprung der modernen Bank als Institution und gebauter Ort sind die Handels- und Messeorte vor allem des mittelalterlichen Italiens. Es waren wohl lombardische Händler, die auf den Märkten Europas ihre Tische = „banca" aufstellten und darauf Münzen und Metalle abwogen, prüften und umtauschten. Der Name „bancheri" = „Bankiers" entstand im 12. Jahrhundert; und die Medici, die Fugger, die Welser, die bedeutendsten Handelsherren und Privatbankiers, dürften nicht mehr bei Regen, Wind und Sonne unter freiem Himmel gesessen haben, um ihrem Beruf nachzugehen.

Die ersten wirklichen Bankbauten wie z. B. 1408 die Casa di San Giorgio in Genua werden nicht so sehr aus Bequemlichkeit oder Repräsentationsgründen errichtet worden sein, sondern weil sich aus dem Geldwechselgeschäft bald auch ein Depositen- und Wechselgeschäft sowie der Giroverkehr entwickelte. Die technischen Voraussetzungen hierfür waren die Entwicklung des Wechsels und des Depositenscheines (Banknote). Diese Menge an Unterlagen konnte ein erfolgreicher Bankier nicht mehr im Säckel am Gürtel tragen; er benötigte ein festes, solides Haus zum Aufbewahren und Schutz solcher Dokumente. Aus dem Ort der sicheren Aufbewahrung wurde der Handels- und Umschlagplatz selbst: die Bank.

Im 15., 16. und 17. Jahrhundert wurde eine ganze Reihe öffentlicher, halböffentlicher und privater Häuser für die an Zahl und Größe ständig zunehmenden Geldgeschäfte gebaut. 1401 eröffnete die eventuell älteste Wechsel-, Depositen- und Girobank in Barcelona, 1609 eine ähnliche in Amsterdam und 1619 die Hamburger Bank in der Hansestadt. Die Bank of England 1694 darf als erste moderne Kreditbank bezeichnet werden.

„Money makes the world go around", lautet eine bekannte Liedzeile aus dem Musical „Cabaret". Doch ist die Geschichte des Geldes und die Erfahrung damit eine vergängliche. Das Gut Geld ist ein flüchtiges; Kriege und Konkurse haben den Menschen gelehrt, daß seine Groschen eine zwar heißbegehrte Sache sind, gleichzeitig aber auch eine höchst unsichere.

Es ist demzufolge mehr als verständlich, daß die ersten veritablen Bankbauten feste, solide Gebäude waren, deren Baugestalt schon rein äußerlich Gediegenheit und Vertrauen vermittelte. Im übrigen nahm man sich die Bautypen zum Vorbild, in denen das Geldgeschäft in den Jahrhunderten vorher floriert hatte: den Tempel, das Kloster, den Palast. Rein sprachlich greifen selbst wir noch heute auf diese Vorgängerbauten zurück, wenn wir von „Palästen des Geldes" sprechen oder abschätzig von „Tempeln des Mammon" („mammon" = aram. für Besitz und Habe, negativ vor allem im Talmud für Geld und Reichtum verwendet).

„Vertrauen ist die Grundlage von allem" ist ein wohlbekannter Slogan der Deutschen Bank. Er faßt alles das zusammen, was Bankbauten bis heute nach außen vermitteln sollen: Gediegenheit und Erfolg.

Die Bank ist eine feste Burg, eine verläßliche Institution, eine monumentale Solidität.

Die Bankbauten im Klassizismus orientierten sich an den antiken Vorbildern des griechischen Tempels oder am römischen Pantheon. Die Börse in St. Petersburg (1801), auf hohem Sockel gelegen und damit aus dem profanen Raum herausgehoben, gleicht im vierseitigen Kranz ihrer schweren Säulen und dem breitgelagerten Giebel dem Parthenon auf der Akropolis in Athen. Das Gebäude der Bank of England von John Soane (1808) nimmt sich im Kuppelraum seiner zentralen Halle die großartige Rotunde des Pantheon in Rom zum Vorbild, welches das Rund des Himmels zitiert.

Der Eintritt in diese geheiligten Hallen des Geldes wird zelebriert. Wer hier eintritt, läßt den schnöden Raum der Straße hinter sich und begibt sich über hohe Stufen und durch breite Portale in eine andere Welt. Auch innen gleichen diese Bauten monumentalen Weihestätten und Heiligtümern: Kassettendecken, schwerer Marmor und Stuck suggerieren die Eigenschaften, die schon Vitruv als Essenz guter Architektur ausmachte, ohne dabei allerdings an Bankbauten zu denken: Standfestigkeit, Nützlichkeit, Schönheit. In dieser Formensprache trifft sich die Repräsentation der Banken mit den Vorstellungen über zuverlässige Sicherheit und Selbstdarstellung ihrer Kunden.

Mit der Ablösung des strengen Klassizismus durch den Historismus begann die Mischung und Nachahmung aller Stile der Baugeschichte. Wie alle repräsentativen Bauten des 19. Jahrhunderts griff auch die Architektur der Banken auf jene bauhistorische Gestalt zurück, die den Eindruck von Harmonie und Unerschütterlichkeit zu vermitteln vermag: vor allem die Renaissance und den Barock. Es ist die erdhafte Schwere und wehrhafte Dauerhaftigkeit dieser Bauten mit ihrem wuchtigen Rusticamauerwerk, die Würde und Feierlichkeit ausstrahlen und damit das Selbstverständnis der Banken widerspiegeln. Die eher filigrane und leicht wirkende Gotik wurde nur selten als Vorbild für Bankgebäude gewählt.

Architektur reflektiert immer die Zeit, in der sie entstanden ist. Mit der Entwicklung neuer Materialien im 19. Jahrhundert wie Beton und Gußeisen und damit der Möglichkeit neuer Konstruktionen wandelten sich die Bankgebäude zu Kathedralen innovativer Architektur. Während außen meist weiter der Eindruck pompöser Feierlichkeit in historischer Gestalt überwog, ließen die Innenräume die schwere Würdearchitektur mit ihren allegorischen Reliefs und klassischen Statuen hinter sich und gewannen die Leichtigkeit von Bahnhofshallen: Große Glaskuppeln überspannen riesige, hohe Kassenhallen, deren lichte Weitläufigkeit mit den über mehrere Geschosse offenen Umgängen, den schmiedeeisernen Gittern, den raffiniert einfachen Tresen und den bunten Glasfenstern den Eindruck transparenter Kathedralen erwecken. Die Bank Credit Lyonnais in Paris, vielleicht einer der schönsten Räume der Jahrhundertwende, erinnert in der großen Spannweite ihres symmetrisch um den Abgang in den Tresor zelebrierten Innenraums an gläserne Gewächshäuser und gigantische Bahnhofshallen.

Mit diesen Verkehrskathedralen teilen die Kassenhallen der Bankgebäude auch die breiten Treppen, die große Uhr, die klaren Einbauten. Gegenüber diesen die großen Spannweiten und neuen Materialien feiernden überwältigenden Räumen ist Otto Wagners Postsparkassenamt in Wien (1906) die sachliche Alternative: außen ein großer Baukörper von ruhigen Linien, innen eine weiße, in ihrer Einfachheit und Übersichtlichkeit fast abstrakt wirkende Kassenhalle. Dieser Raum macht keinerlei Verbeugung in Richtung der Geschichte oder der bis dahin bekannten und bevorzugten Repräsentation von Banken. Ebenso reduziert in Farben und Formen wie elegant in der Schnörkellosigkeit der Halle und der Schmucklosigkeit der großen Glasdecke zeigt sich hier eine neue moderne Form der Repräsentation, die in der darauffolgenden Zeit allerdings nur wenige Anhänger finden sollte.

Die zwanziger Jahre, die Hoch-Zeit der Avantgarde und Moderne in der Architektur, waren eine Zeit wirtschaftlicher Baisse. Börsenkräche und Inflationen ließen das Geldgewerbe nicht an innovative Neubauten denken. Insofern entstand in dieser Zeit kaum ein bemerkens- und erwähnenswertes modernes Bankgebäude.

Unter den nach dem Zweiten Weltkrieg errichteten Bauten sind es vor allem die neuen Bankgebäude, deren ruhige und einfache Formen die Sprache der Moderne sprechen. Die gebaute Machtgebärde der alten Bankhäuser gehörte nun der Vergangenheit an; die Bank entschied sich für sachliche Repräsentation und gegen ehrfurchtgebietende Würdeformeln. Im Zuge des massenhaften Bauens verkam das einfache Bauen jedoch schnell zu einfallsloser Ärmlichkeit. In der gesichtslosen Rasterarchitektur der sechziger und siebziger Jahre unterschied sich das Bankgebäude in nichts von anderen vulgärfunktionalistischen Gebäuden. Die Vereinheitlichung im Bauen hat in dieser Zeit auch die Banken eingeholt.

In die Kritik an der autogerechten Stadt schlossen wütende und protestierende Studenten in den siebziger Jahren auch und vor allem die Banken ein. Kritik und Mißtrauen wurden besonders durch zwei Erscheinungen ausgelöst. Das eine ist die Architektur der verspiegelten Fassaden, die sich scheinbar offen gibt, gleichwohl aber Menschen und Stadt auf Distanz hält und sich ihnen gegenüber abschottet. Das andere ist die Tendenz von Banken, größer, höher und weiter hinauf in den Himmel zu bauen und in Hochhäusern eine neue zeichenhafte Identität zu gewinnen. Die Hochhäuser der siebziger und achtziger Jahre sind in ihrer Mehrheit banale Solitäre, ebenso gesichts- wie maßstabslos. Der Bürger, der Kunde der Banken, fühlt sich durch sie eher abgestoßen als umworben, eher verunsichert als bürgernah angesprochen. Aus vielen dieser Bauten spricht Arroganz, nicht aber Vertrauenswürdigkeit. Eine frühe Ausnahme ist die international bekannte Hongkong und Shanghai Bank von Norman Foster, die durch ihre eigenwillige und einprägsame Gestalt zum Wahrzeichen des Hongkong der achtziger Jahre wurde.

Wie die Wirtschaft haben in den letzten Jahren auch die Banken die Botschaft, die Architektur darstellt, wiederentdeckt. Im Zuge der Diskussion über corporate identity überdenkt man auch wieder die eigene gebaute Gestalt und ihre Wirkung. Die moderne Bank ist ein reines Dienstleistungsunternehmen, als Arbeitsplatz nach innen so wichtig wie in der Außenwirkung für die Stadt. Stand früher das Gespräch mit dem Kunden im Mittelpunkt des Bankgeschäftes, ist heute Selbstbedienung wie im Supermarkt angesagt; das Gespräch am Schalter wird durch neue Medien ersetzt, der Ort der vertrauten Erörterung über Geldangelegenheiten ist zur Technikzentrale geworden.

Die Konsequenzen für die Architektur der Banken sind so vielfältig und uneinheitlich wie das gesamte Spektrum des (post-)modernen Bauens. Der gestalterische Ausdruck der neuen Bankhäuser reicht von den schwingenden organischen Formen der Nederlandsche Middenstandsbank in Amsterdam (Alberts, van Huut, 1987) bis zu der exzentrischen Staatsbank in Fribourg (Mario Botta, 1982), von der hintersinnigen gigantischen Stadtvilla der Landeszentralbank in Potsdam (Ortner + Ortner, 1996) bis zu dem nackten, rationalistischen Kubus der Landeszentralbank in Leipzig (Hans Kollhoff, 1996).

Viele dieser Bauten entstehen in Vororten oder am Rande der Zentren. In den Innenstädten ist für Neubauten nur noch selten Platz. Hier nisten sich Banken nicht selten in Altbauten ein und leisten mit deren denkmalgerechtem Umbau und maßstäblichen Anbauten einen Beitrag zur Erhaltung eines ortstypischen Stadtbildes. So wie dies bei der Deutschen Bank in Essen der Fall ist.

Ingeborg Flagge

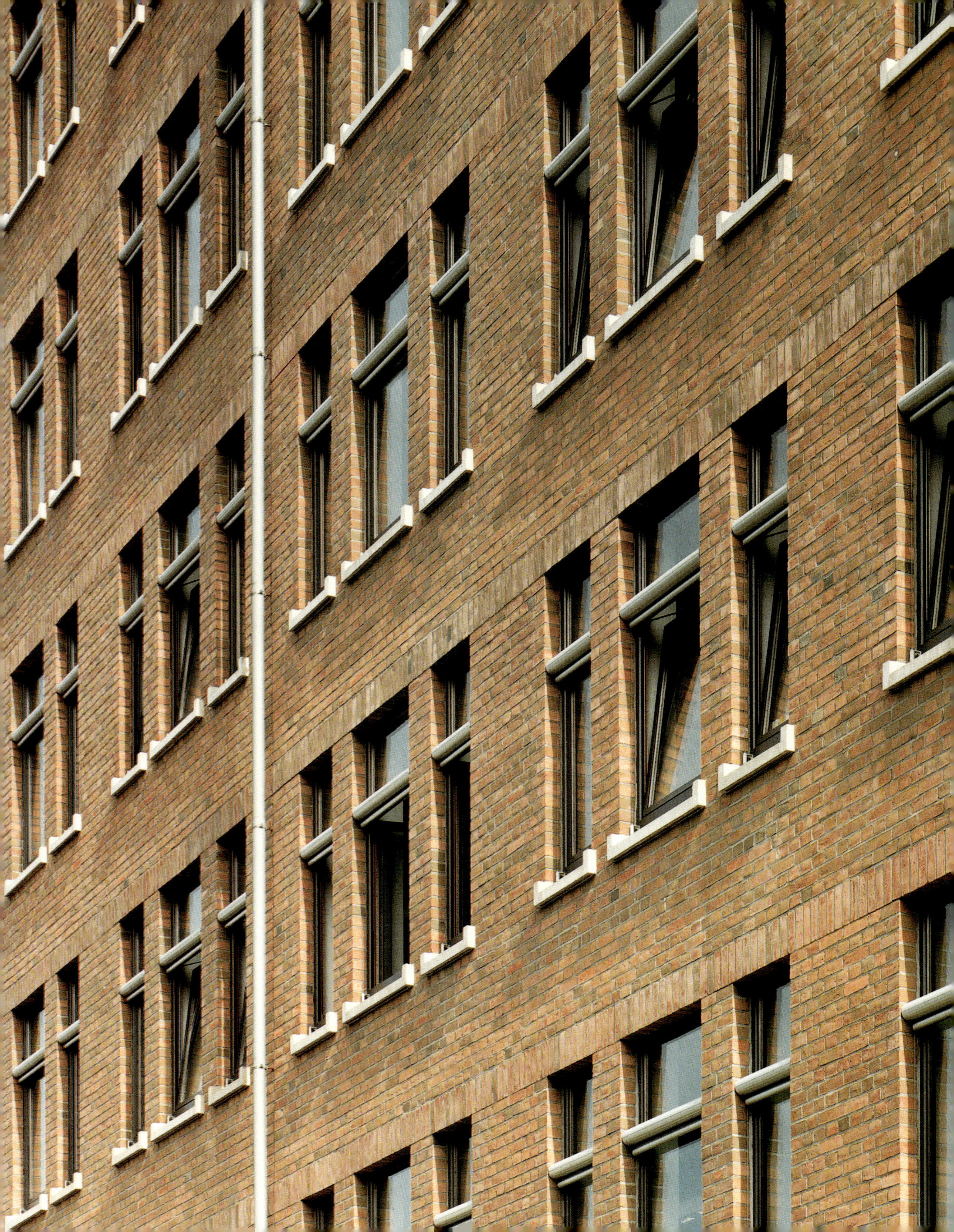

Foto: Neuhaus, Duisburg

Renovierung und Neubau der Deutschen Bank Essen, 1993–1997

Wird die Aufgabe der heutigen Architektur innerhalb der Dichte der Stadt als Bestandteil eines Erhaltungsprozesses, einer Schichtung, einer partiellen Erneuerung und, in einigen Fällen, eines Abrisses verstanden, so sind Bauaufgaben wie die der Renovierung und des Neubaus der Deutschen Bank in Essen geradezu Indikatoren für die inhaltliche und gestalterische Sensibilität, mit der Bauherren und Architekten an solche Vorhaben herangehen. Das Bewußtsein, daß heute nicht alles von Grund auf neu gebaut werden muß, ja gebaut werden kann, bestimmt zunehmend die Haltung, d. h. die inhaltliche und gestalterische Sensibilität der beim Bau verantwortlichen Beteiligten.

Wie wurde doch in den sechziger und siebziger Jahren mit der Bausubstanz umgegangen; hohe Räume aus der Jahrhundertwende wurden durch abgehängte Decken dem horizontalen Raumgeschmack angepaßt; die vom Zweiten Weltkrieg noch übriggebliebenen Stuckdetails wurden dem bevorzugten Reinheitsideal der klassischen Moderne geopfert; die überkommenen einfachen Raumwirkungen und klar strukturierten Raumfolgen wurden durch bewußt anti-achsiale Wegeführungen aufgelöst.

Einige dieser Veränderungsmaßnahmen mußte auch das 1901 von Peter Zindel für die 1872 gegründete Essener Creditanstalt errichtete Eckgebäude an der Maxstraße und Lindenallee, welches 1908 von Wilhelm Mertens in Richtung Lindenstraße erweitert wurde, in den Jahren 1971–1975 erleben. Mertens, der auch der Architekt der Berliner Zentrale der Deutschen Bank war, verstand es, den ursprünglich auf einer diagonalen Achse basierenden Bau Zindels mit einem bausprachlich der Eckrotunde angeglichenen Mittelrisalit als neue Einheit zu erweitern. Der hiermit fast unmittelbar unternommene Anbau Mertens – knapp sieben Jahre lagen zwischen den beiden Bautätigkeiten – läßt die Bedenken der heutigen, äußerst kritischen Einstellung gegenüber einer direkten Übernahme der Architektursprache im Falle einer Erweiterung nicht zu. Die Einheit des Bauwerks war damals wie heute oberstes Ziel der Architekten und Bauherren.

Ebenso wie die Einheit der Fassaden von Mertens gesucht wurde, war die räumliche Durchdringung von Inhalt zur Fassade für Zindel und Mertens maßgeblich. Daß die Großzügigkeit der Palastarchitektur Zindels mit den über sechs Meter hohen Vorstandsbüros auf der Ebene des Erdgeschosses von der Straßen- bis auf die Hofseite durchgeführt wurde, dürfte schon für Mertens ein gestalterisches Problem gewesen sein. So stufte er über rückseitige Treppenanlagen die Raumhöhen der repräsentativen Etagen von jeweils sechseinhalb und fünf Metern auf knapp über drei Meter ab und verdoppelte dadurch die Zahl der Geschosse im Vergleich zu Zindels straßenseitiger Ausnutzung.

1925 übernahm die Deutsche Bank das Gebäude. Von der ursprünglich geschickten Raumstruktur Zindels und Mertens blieb nach den Kriegsschäden und der umfangreichen Renovierung in den frühen siebziger Jahren nichts mehr übrig. In den frühen neunziger Jahren wurde die mittlerweile entstandene

Ansammlung von unterschiedlich geplanten Abschnitten mit ihren jeweils eigenen Raumhöhen und den damit zusammenhängenden Niveauunterschieden den Nutzern bewußt, so daß eine grundlegende Neustrukturierung mit den mittlerweile auch wieder notwendig gewordenen, altersbedingten Instandhaltungsmaßnahmen durchgeführt werden mußte. Genaue Kostenvergleiche zwischen umfangreichen Sanierungs- und Neubaumaßnahmen unterstützten die Entscheidung zugunsten eines weitgehenden Neubaus unter Beibehaltung der noch übriggebliebenen denkmalgeschützten Fassaden Zindels und Mertens. (Die Kosten einer umfangreichen Sanierung wurden bei einer bestehenden Hauptnutzungsfläche von 6.671 m^2 auf DM 47,6 Mill. geschätzt, gegenüber 76 Mill. für einen weitgehenden Neubau mit einer neuen Hauptnutzungsfläche von 8.600 m^2, also einem Flächenzuwachs von knapp 30%.)

Infolge der Überlegungen zur Neustrukturierung wurden viele Anläufe genommen, um optimale Lösungen zu finden. Beschränkte Wettbewerbe und Gutachterverfahren wurden in den frühen neunziger Jahren durchgeführt und ermöglichten einen allmählichen Prozeß der Nutzungsdefinition des zukünftigen Gebäudes. So erwies sich der polygonale Grundstückszuschnitt wie auch die vorhandene Fassade als eigentliche Herausforderung an die geladenen Architekten. Nach der langwierigen Suche nach einer in jeder Hinsicht optimalen Lösung gelang es dem Bauherrn mit Unterstützung des Architekturbeirates (dem Thomas Herzog, Vittorio Magnago Lampugnani und der Verfasser angehören), dem Bauvorschlag von Wilhelm Kücker zuzustimmen. Das Bauvorhaben wurde den Nutzern nach vierjähriger Planungs- und Bauzeit termingerecht übergeben.

Wilhelm Kückers Entwurf geht in der Grunddisposition von einer selbstverständlichen Lösung aus, die, im nachhinein betrachtet, eine verblüffende Einfachheit hat, die aber allen seinen Vorgängern verborgen geblieben zu sein scheint.

Die erste dominante Entscheidung bezieht sich auf die Idealisierung von Hofstrukturen, sei es die diagonalsymmetrische Wiederherstellung des Eckvolumens des ehemaligen Zindel-Baus oder die erstmalige logische Vervollkommnung des Mertens-Blocks. Kücker scheut dabei keine grundstücksbedingten Winkel. Diese beeinträchtigen aber weder die innere Raumabfolge noch die Klarheit der baukörperlichen Erscheinung. So wird die Erweiterung an der Maxstraße konsequent jenem Straßenzug angepaßt, wie sich auch der westliche Flügel der Grundstücksgrenze genau anfügt, so daß durch eine eventuelle zukünftige Verlängerung dieses Flügels in Richtung Maxstraße eine Arrondierung der Gesamtanlage entstehen könnte.

Der Entwurf Wilhelm Kückers hat es verstanden, die durch die Eckrotunde vorgegebene städtebauliche wie architektonische Spannung mit einer großzügigen Kassenhalle aufzulösen. Hinter dieser im heutigen Stadtbild Essens einmaligen und repräsentativen Kuppel ist tatsächlich ein Raum entstanden, der das Versprechen von Repräsentation inhaltlich und räumlich hält. Mag sein, daß die Erwartungen vieler Bürger und Nutzer dieses Bankgebäudes überhöht, vielleicht sogar ein wenig unzeitgemäß sind – denn welche Bank benötigt heute noch eine tatsächliche Kassenhalle, sind doch die Bargeldautomaten meist im Windfang untergebracht; aber es sind nun einmal diese Unterschiede zwischen den einzelnen Institutionen, die die einen zu einer Bewahrung gewisser Traditionen verpflichtet und die den kulturellen Unterschied darstellen, den gewisse Kunden bewußt oder unterbewußt bevorzugen, und die die anderen zu der rationalistischen Konsequenz anleiten, die ihrerseits eine kühle, ja manchmal auch abweisende Abstraktion ausstrahlt.

Foto: Neuhaus, Duisburg

Gewiß ist die Kassenhalle mit ihren an Fabrikbauten aus der Region erinnernden Stahlportalen ein Luxus aus der Sicht der Bauherrenschaft, aber im Gesamtverhältnis zum umbauten Raum ist ihre Wirkung größer als ihre Kosten. Auch in dieser Hinsicht hat die Halle ein Vielfaches erreicht.

So gestaltet der Bestand unter bewußter Rücksichtnahme auf die in ihn gesetzten Erwartungen auch den Neubau mit. Die Rolle der Kassenhalle ist paradigmatisch für alle bis in das kleinste Detail gehenden Bezüge zwischen Alt und Neu. Ein Durchschreiten der Räume läßt die Beziehungen zwischen den rhythmisch räumlichen Vorgaben der denkmalgeschützten Fassade und den neuen Büros und Gemeinschaftseinrichtungen erfahrbar werden.

Hinter den alten Fassaden finden sich nicht nach ihren Eigengesetzlichkeiten angeordnete Geschosse, keine respektlosen, die alten Fensteröffnungen durchschneidenden, prall mit Technik aufgeladenen Fußböden. Wilhelm Kückers Entwurf sieht vielmehr auch hier eine direkte wie einfache Lösung vor, die auf die grandiosen vorhandenen Raumdimensionen eingeht, um sie mittels einer ebenso großartigen neuen Treppenanlage auf die neue, normale Geschoßstruktur einzustimmen.

Diese ungewöhnliche Doppeltreppenanlage bildet eine durchsichtige Raumschicht zwischen den hohen, straßenseitigen, erdgeschossigen Räumen und den beiden der Kassenhalle zugewandten Galerien. Letztere werden dank der zurückversetzten und zum Teil verglasten Besprechungskabinen als ebenso transparente Räume verstanden. Es ist mit all diesen Elementen eine kontinuierliche Raumqualität entstanden, die von außen durch die steinerne Fassade zunächst nicht vermutet wird, aber den Betrachter deshalb um so mehr anspricht. Die Kombination von verblüffend einfacher Raumlösung und offener Raumqualität ist im Vergleich mit der sonstigen heutigen Architektur erfrischend.

Ohne die respektvolle Erhaltung der Vorgaben durch den Bestand wäre diese Renovierung und Revitalisierung nicht gelungen. Ein Rückblick auf die vielen Entwürfe von Kückers Vorgängern bis zurück zu Zindel und Mertens macht deutlich, daß der jetzige Zustand eine Qualität erreicht hat, die zu keiner Zeit vorher existierte, weder als tatsächlicher baulicher Zustand noch als angedachter Entwurf, so daß man vom jetzigen Bauwerk behaupten darf, daß es nicht nur eine absolute Verbesserung gegenüber den vorherigen Zuständen darstellt, sondern daß es mit seiner Raumqualität und Typologie beispielhaft in die Architekturgeschichte eingehen wird.

Zahlreiche potentielle innenräumliche Konflikte wurden von Kücker mit einer zurückhaltenden Leichtigkeit gelöst, so zum Beispiel die Neugestaltung der Eingangsbereiche in der Eckrotunde und im Mittelrisalit. Da die alte Eingangsebene oberhalb des Souterrains lag, diese aber auf verständlichen Wunsch des Bauherrn auf das Straßenniveau abgesenkt wurde, mußte die Treppenanlage im Mittelrisalit völlig neugestaltet werden. Sowohl die neuen riesigen Türen als auch die symmetrische Treppenanlage entsprechen in ihrer Materialität, handwerklichen Anfertigungen und in ihren Ausmaßen der in der alten Fassade ausgedrückten Haltung. Fein verarbeitetes Messing und schönes Eichenholz für die Türen, selbstverständlich geschwungen behandelter Marmor sowie angemessen großzügige Emporen geben dem Eingangs- und Erschließungsbereich eine noble Atmosphäre. Sie ist nicht übertrieben, denn ihr ist es zu verdanken, daß ein verständlicher Übergang von Außen nach Innen, von großstädtischer Straßenfront bis zu zeitgenössischen Einzelbüros, erreicht werden konnte.

Auch die Geschäftsleitung kommt in den Genuß des Respekts vor dem Tradierten. Das piano nobile des ehemaligen zweiten Geschosses wurde auf der Straßenseite ebenso von fensterdurchschneidenen Fußböden verschont wie auch das untere Geschoß. Die Filialdirektoren der Bank bleiben auch nach dem Umbau auf dieser Ebene. Darüber, hinter der Attika, ordnete Kücker Gemeinschaftsräume zwischen Atrien an. Die Cafeteria und die Schulungsräume erhalten dadurch Tageslicht und Ausblicke in den Straßenraum.

Ist Wilhelm Kücker die Erhaltung der denkmalgeschützten Straßenfassade ohne Bruch gegenüber dem dahinterliegenden Innenraum gelungen, so gab es für ihn noch weitere schwierige Nutzungsvorgaben. Die neuen Büroflächen sollten flexibel genutzt werden können. Für den Fall, daß der Eigenbedarf der Bank nicht die Gesamtfläche umfaßte, sollte eine weitere separate Erschließung angeboten werden. Da der repräsentative Charakter der Zugänge von der Ecke Maxstraße und Lindenallee und vom Mittelrisalit an der Lindenallee eine Fremdnutzung aber eigentlich ausschloß, entwarf Wilhelm Kücker einen durchgehenden hofseitigen Zugang, der notfalls auch von der Feuerwehr benutzt werden kann. Dieser Zugang hat einen so öffentlichen Charakter, daß bei einer Fremdnutzung der Bürofläche kein Gefühl des Hinterhofs aufkommt.

Darf man bei diesem Bauvorhaben allgemein von einer geglückten Synthese von vorhandener Substanz und anspruchsvollen neuen Vorgaben sprechen, so kann man die neue Fassade in der Maxstraße – in Erweiterung von Zindels Südfassade – vielleicht als den äußeren Ausdruck dieser allgemeinen Synthese und als Lackmustest der Fähigkeit des Architekten ansehen. Und auch hier gelingt es Kücker, dem Neuen eine sowohl verbindende als auch eigenständige Qualität zu geben.

Horizontal gegliedertes Mauerwerk umschließt die eingestellte Stahlrahmenkonstruktion. In ihr wird die rhythmische und räumliche Struktur des Neubaus ausgedrückt. Eine Differenzierung der Füllung innerhalb dieses Stahlrahmens deutet aber wiederum auf die benachbarte grobe und feine Rustika. Die im Neubau bündig vorgeblendete grobe Schichtung des Füllwerks entspricht der tiefen Rustika des Erdgeschosses, die zurückversetzte Füllung des neuen dritten und vierten Obergeschosses mit der nun freistehenden Rundstütze korrespondiert mit der Säulenordnung des ersten Obergeschosses des Zindel-Baus. Auch die Rundöffnungen im Vierendeel-Balken, der die Garagen- und Feuerwehrzufahrt überbrückt, stellen ein Echo der Rundbögen der Nachbarfassade dar. Dieser Vierendeel-Balken löst gleichsam auch die Versprechen der modernen Architektur ein: befreiende Raumwirkung und Verdichtung der historischen Erfahrungen.

Die drei Rundfenster sind zugleich Ausgangspunkt und Schlußlicht für die Gesamtanlage. Sie sind wie der Gesamtentwurf eine glückliche Zusammenfassung angemessener Lösungsansätze, die funktionelle Bedürfnisse und repräsentative Erwartungen gleichwertig vereint.

Waren die Befürchtungen am Anfang der Überlegungen zur Renovierung des Bankgebäudes groß, haben die vielen architektonischen Entwürfe in der Zwischenzeit die Bauherrenschaft eher verunsichert als in ihrer Haltung bestärkt, so darf man heute dem Bauherren um so mehr für seine Beharrlichkeit in der Suche nach dieser Lösung, den Ausführenden für ihre handwerklichen Leistungen, dem Architekten und seinem Team für seine beispielhafte Lösung gratulieren. Nicht immer wird, was lange währt, auch gut. Aber in diesem Fall wird das Sprichwort seiner inhaltlichen Bedeutung gerecht.

Wilfried Wang

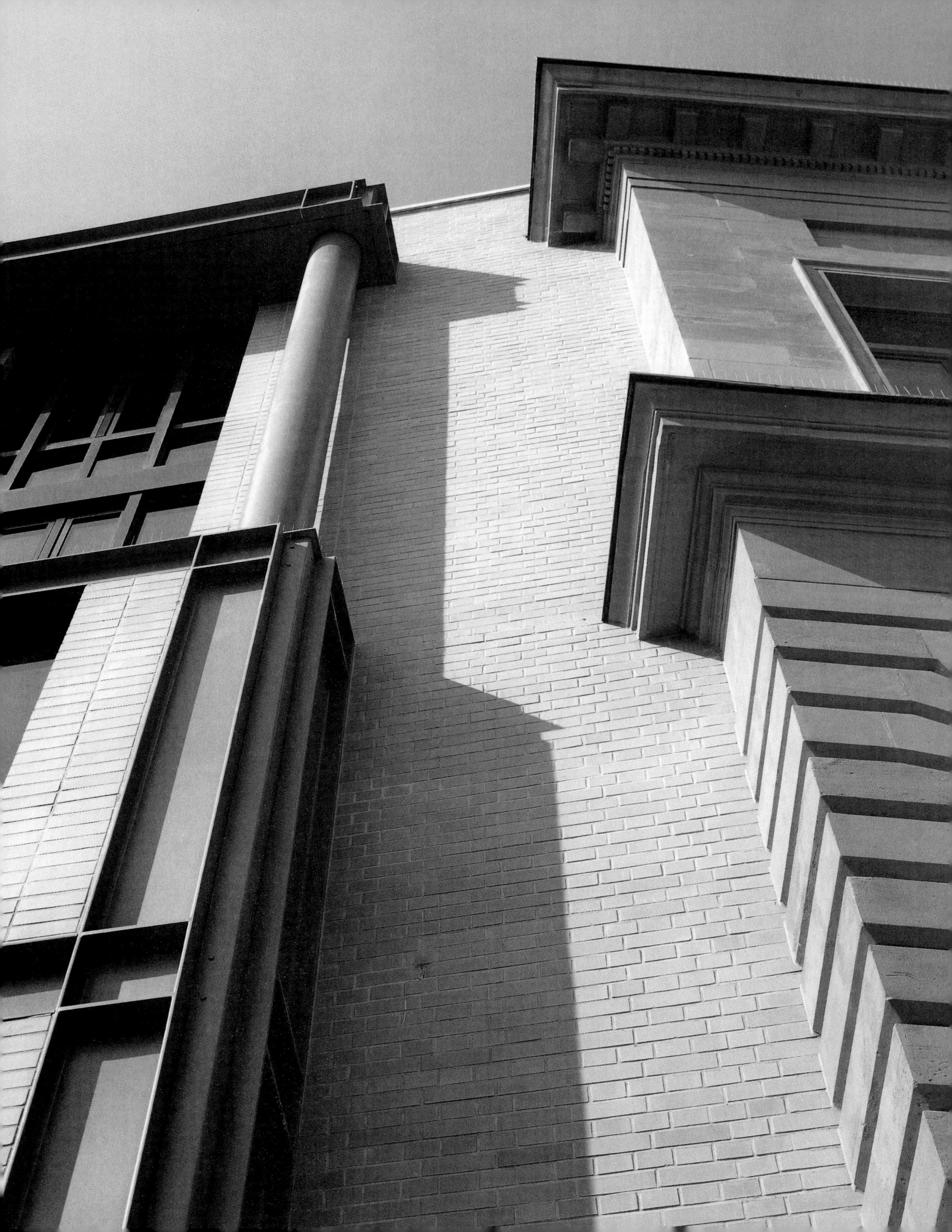

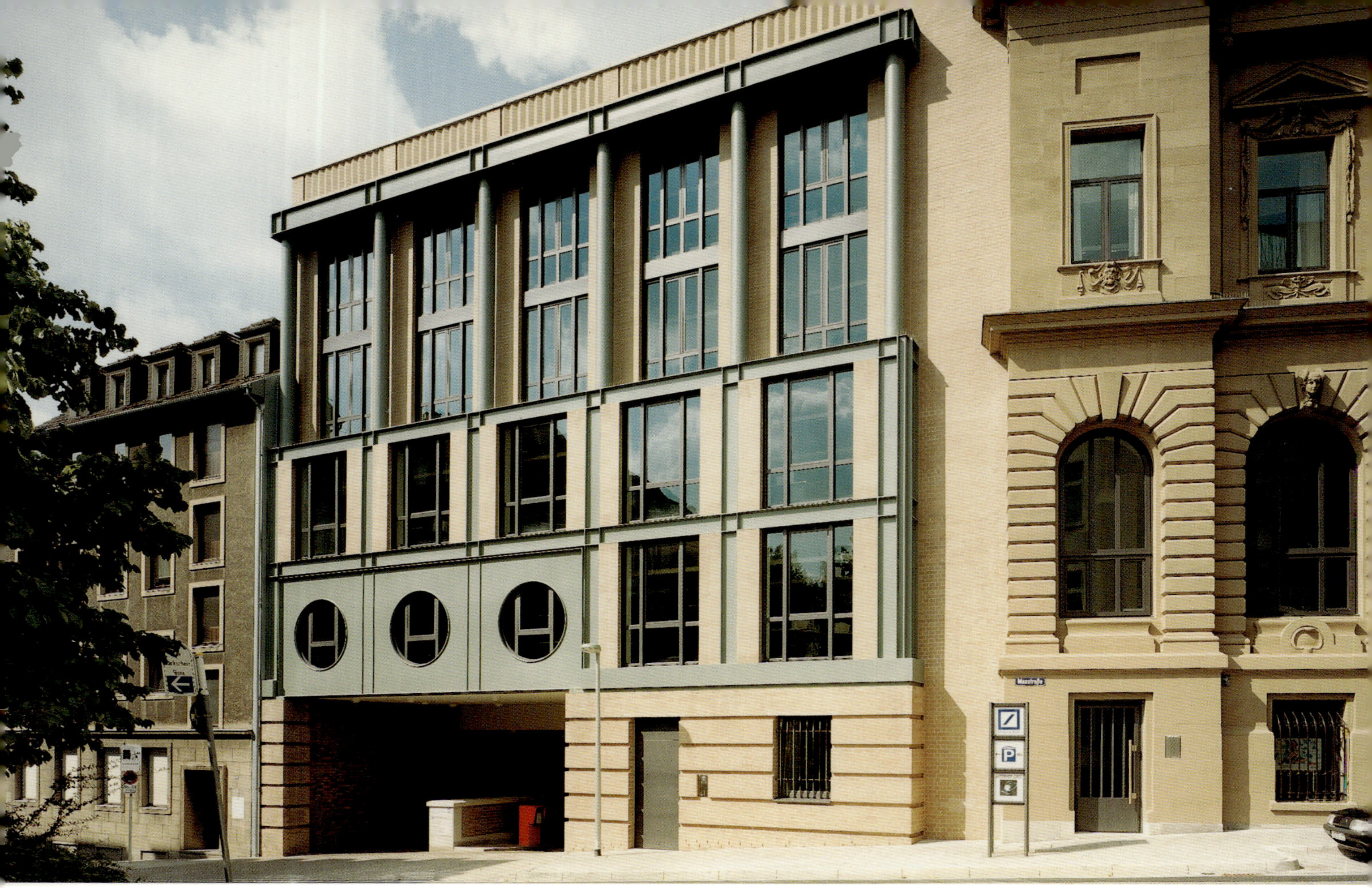

Fassade Maxstrasse

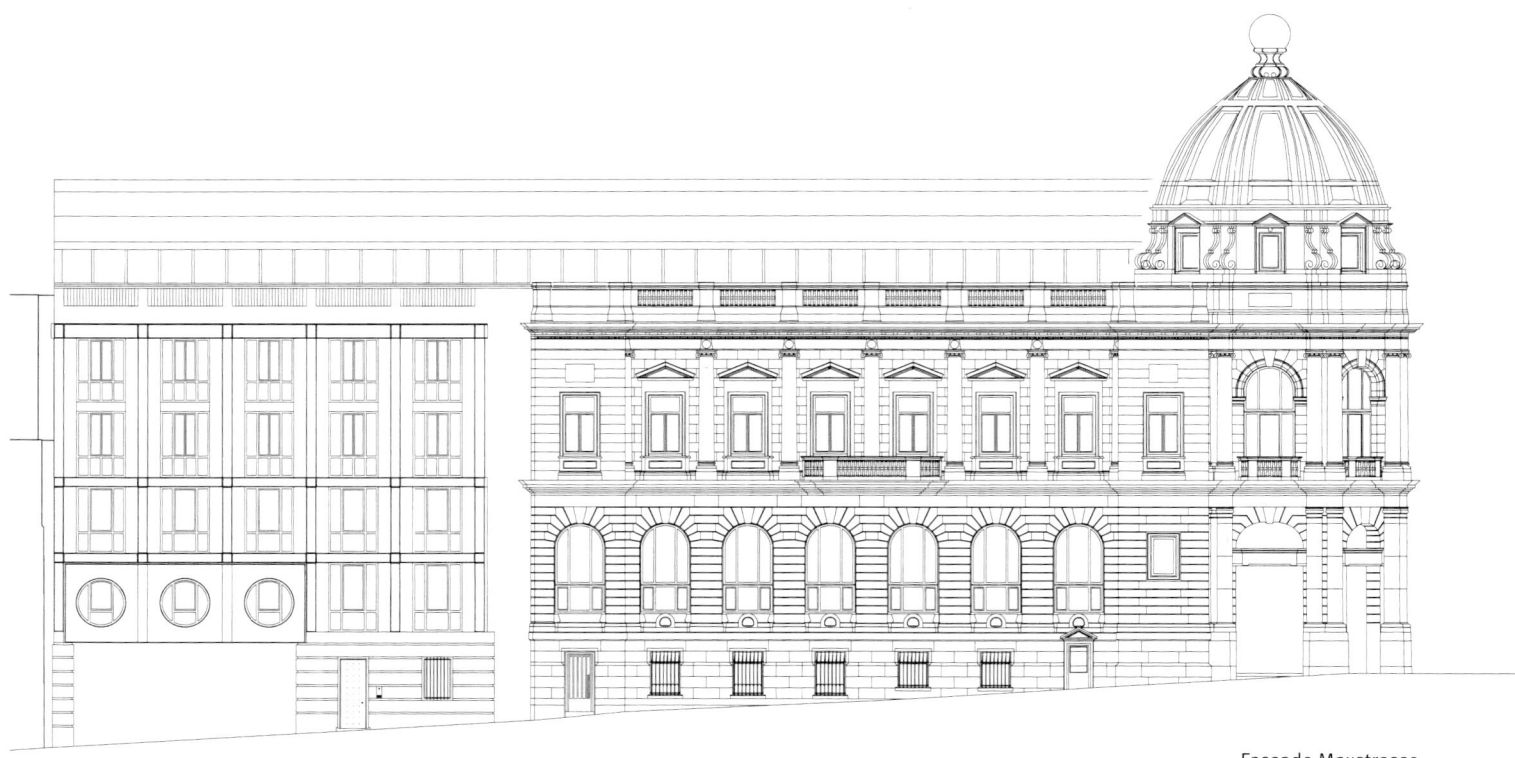

Fassade Maxstrasse

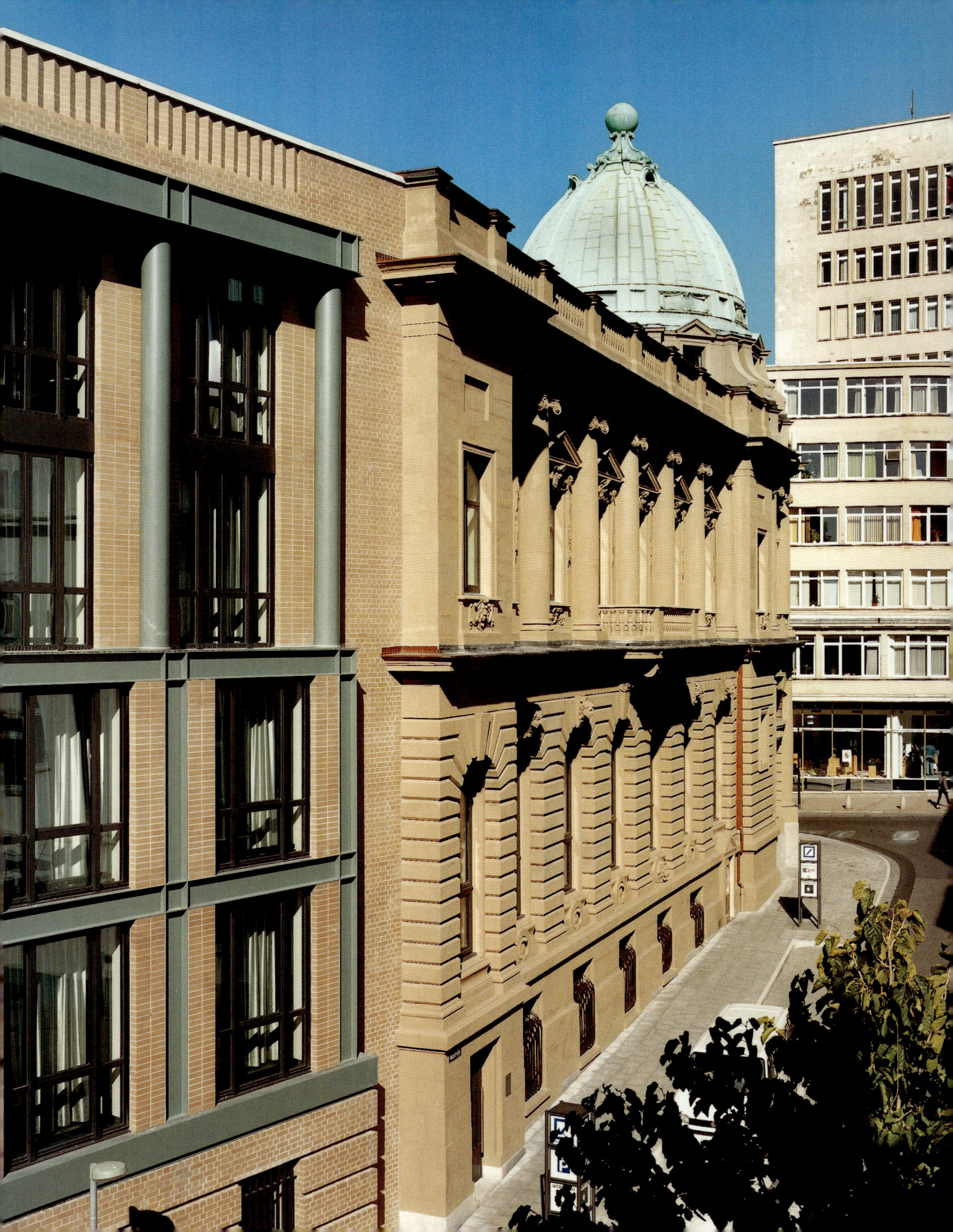

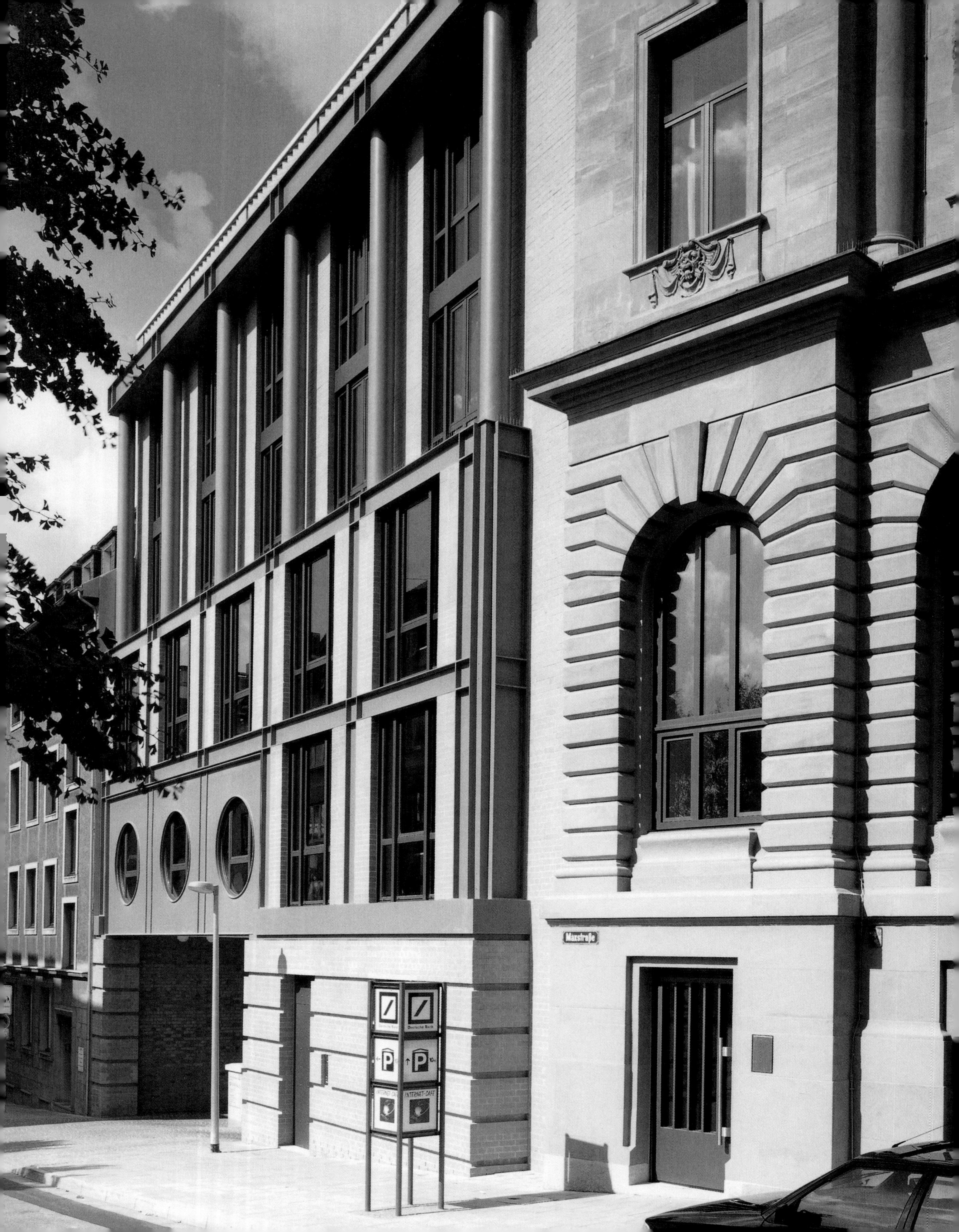
Maxstraße
Deutsche Bank
P
INTERNET-CAFE

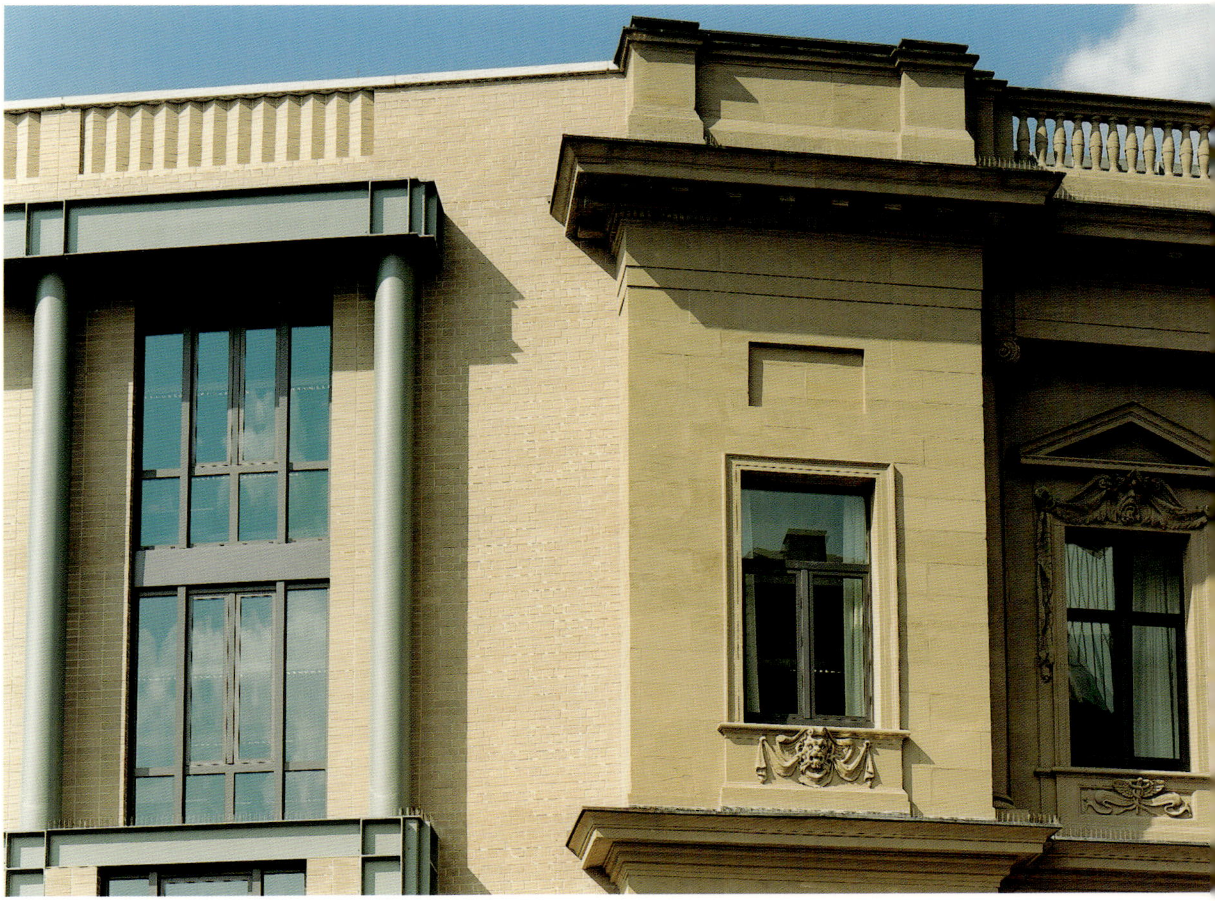

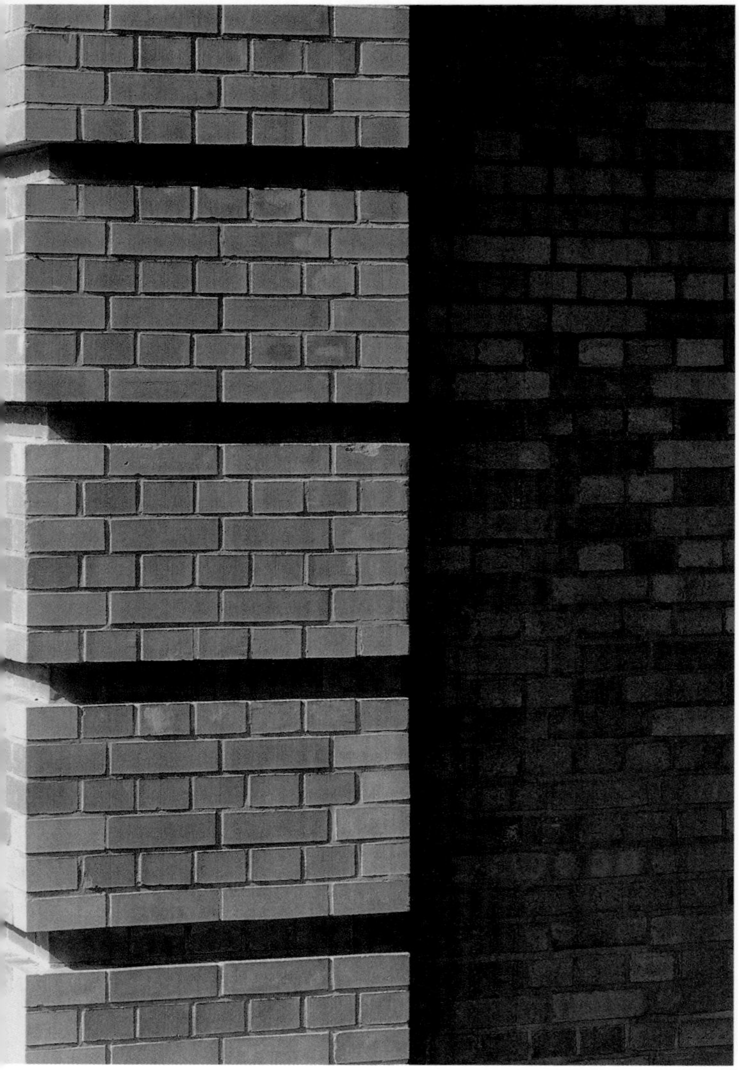

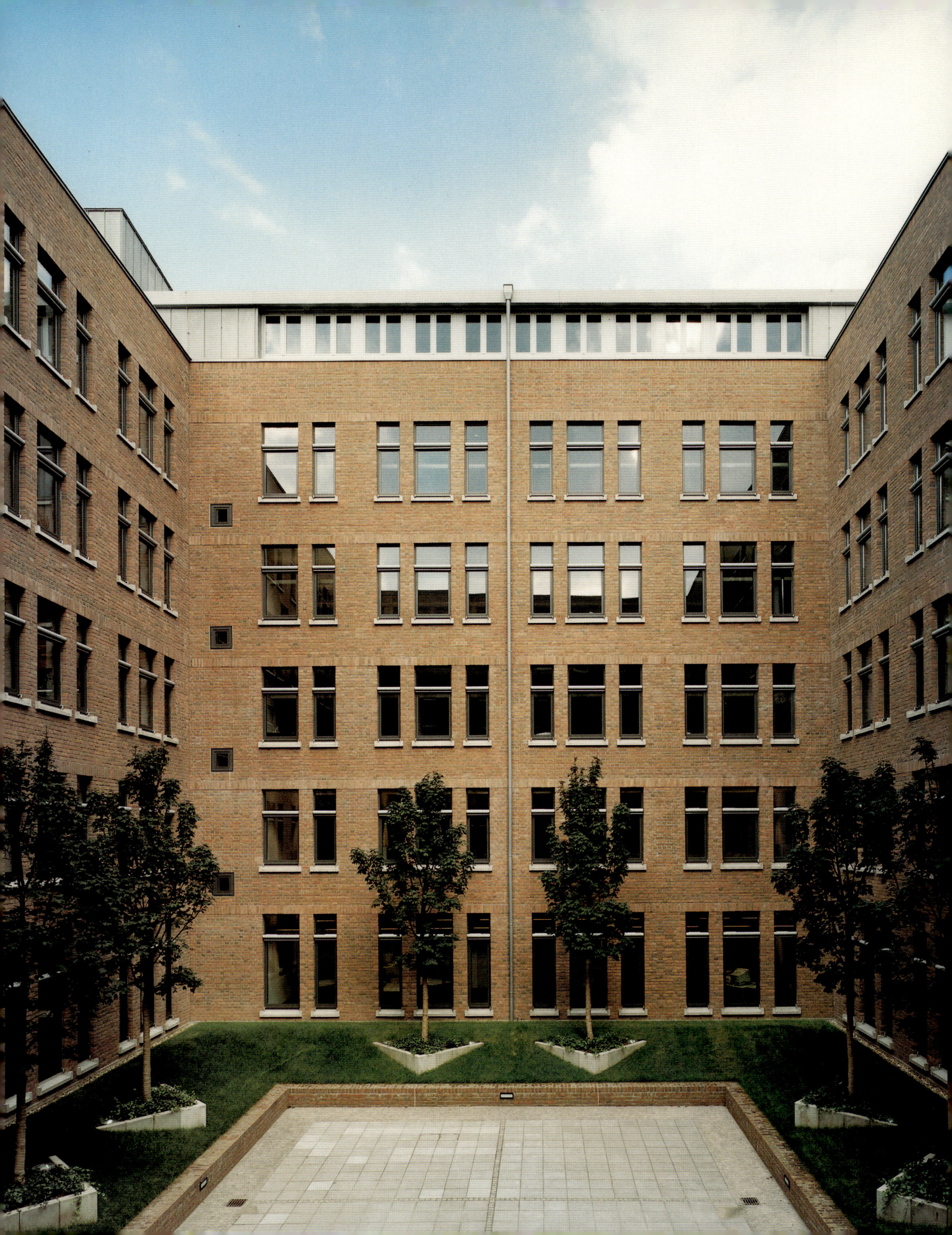

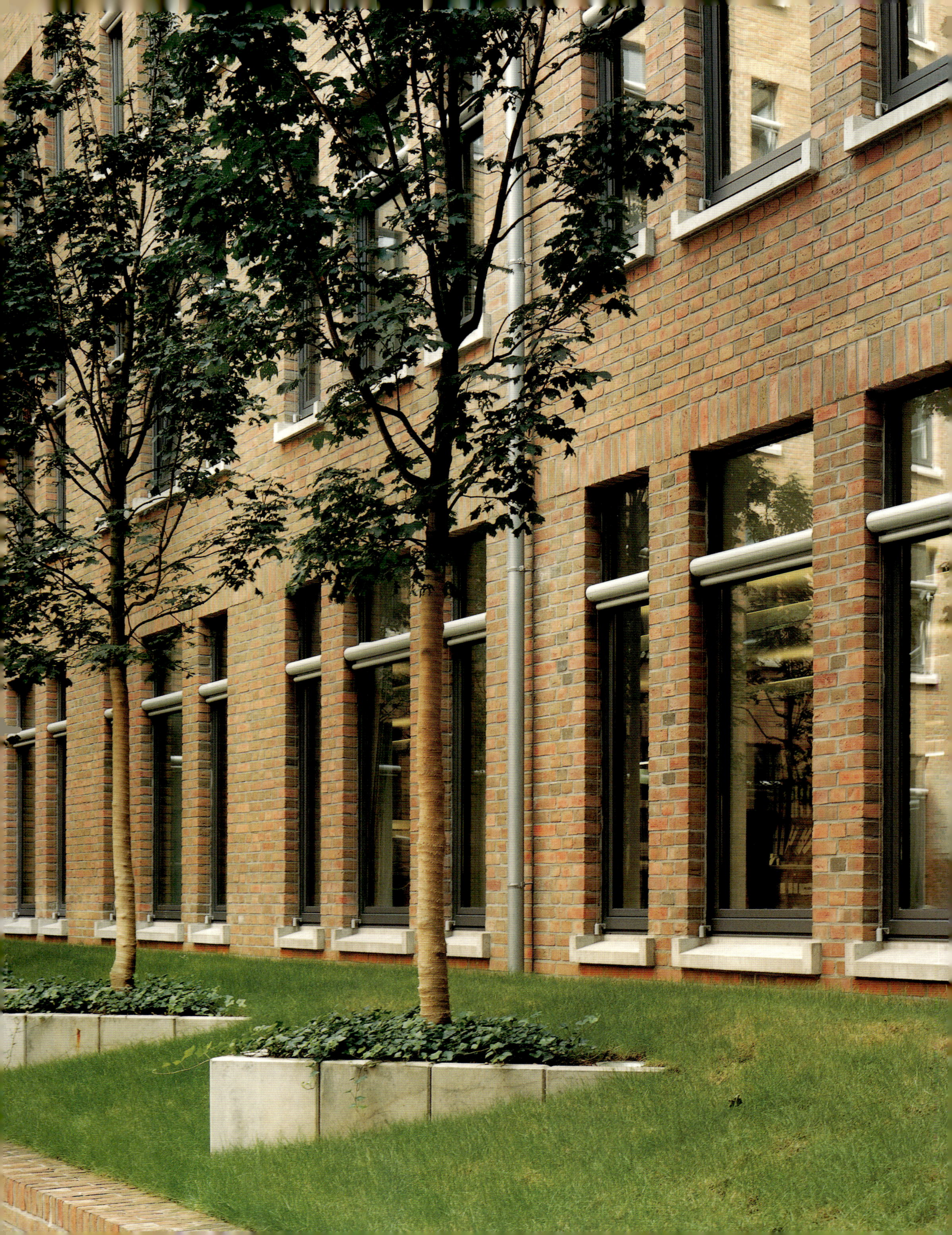

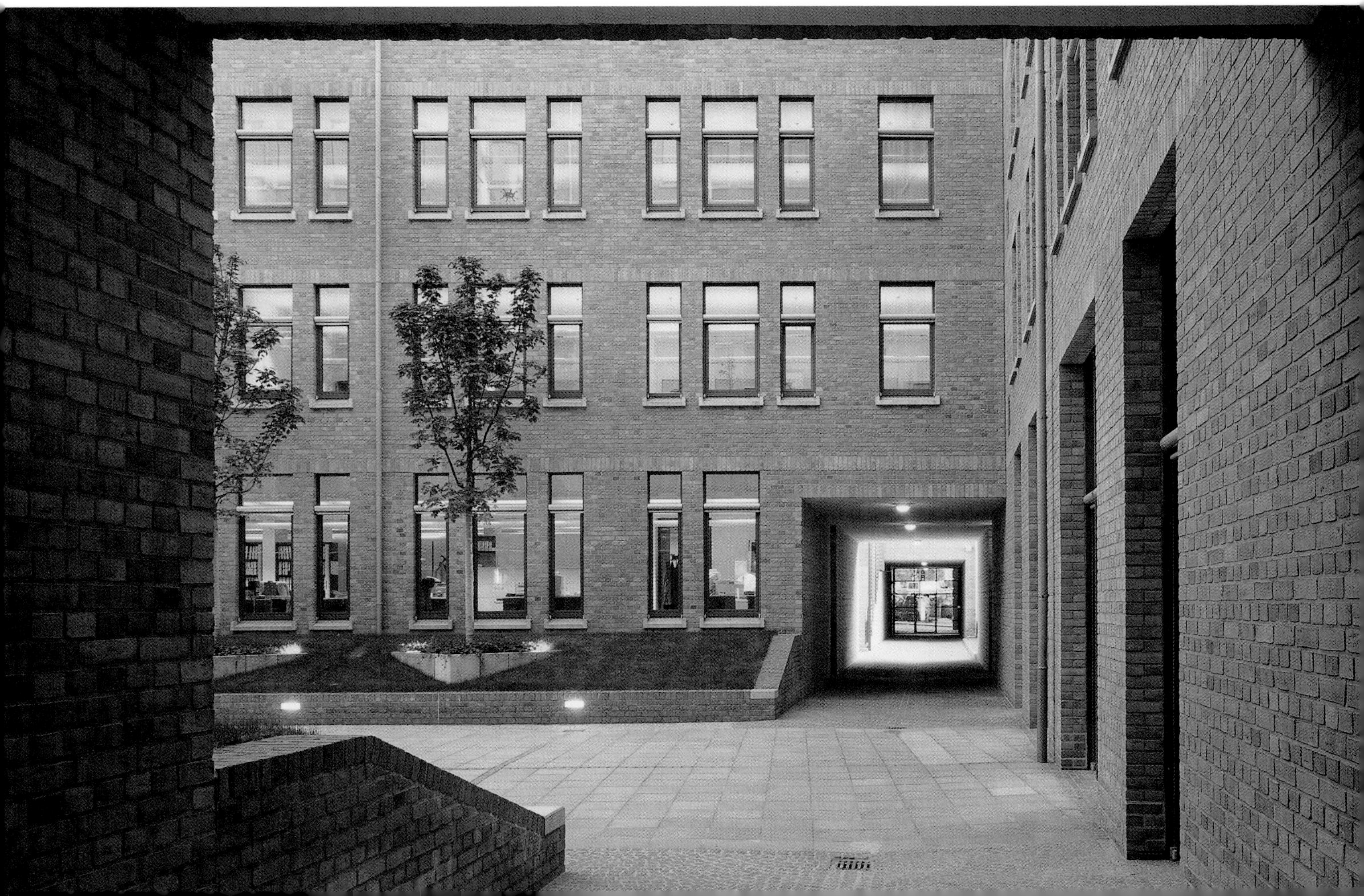

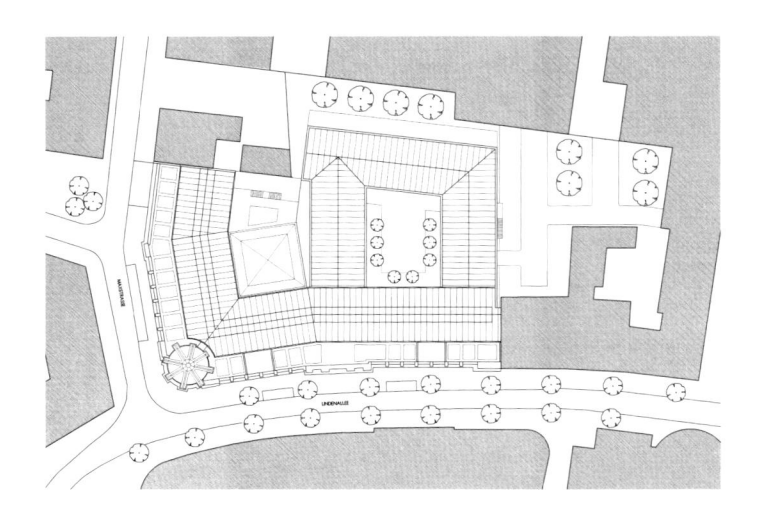

Lageplan – M 1:2000

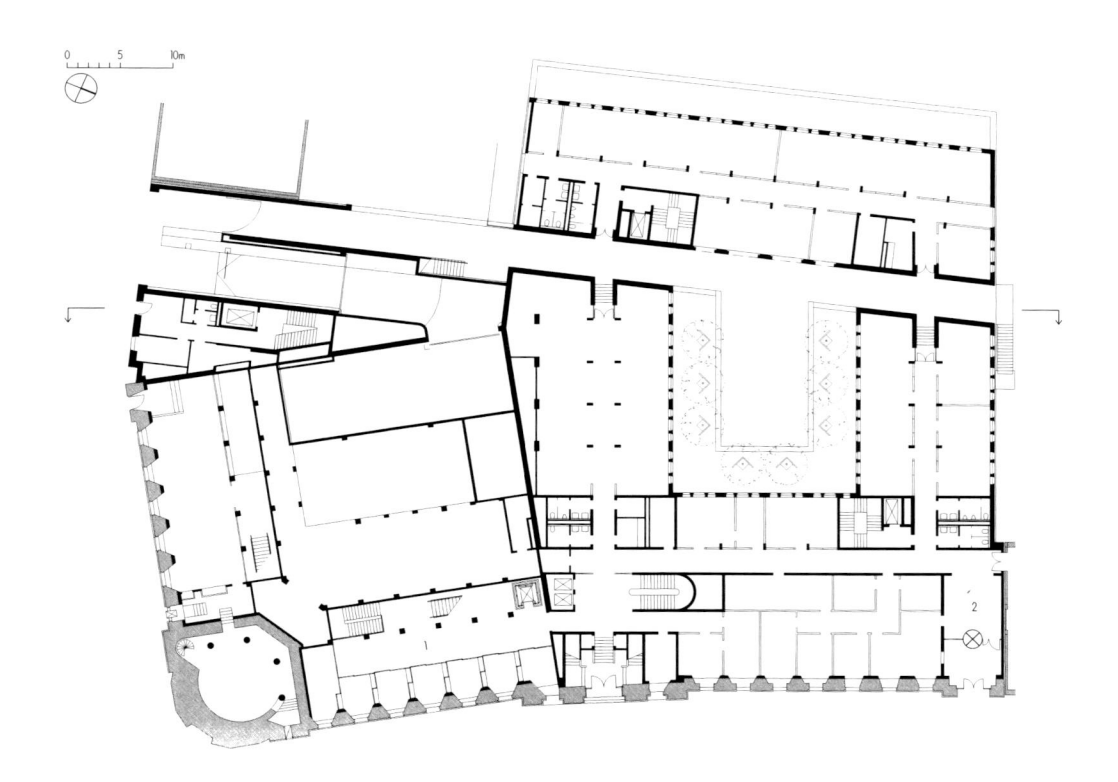

1. Erdgeschoß – M 1:750

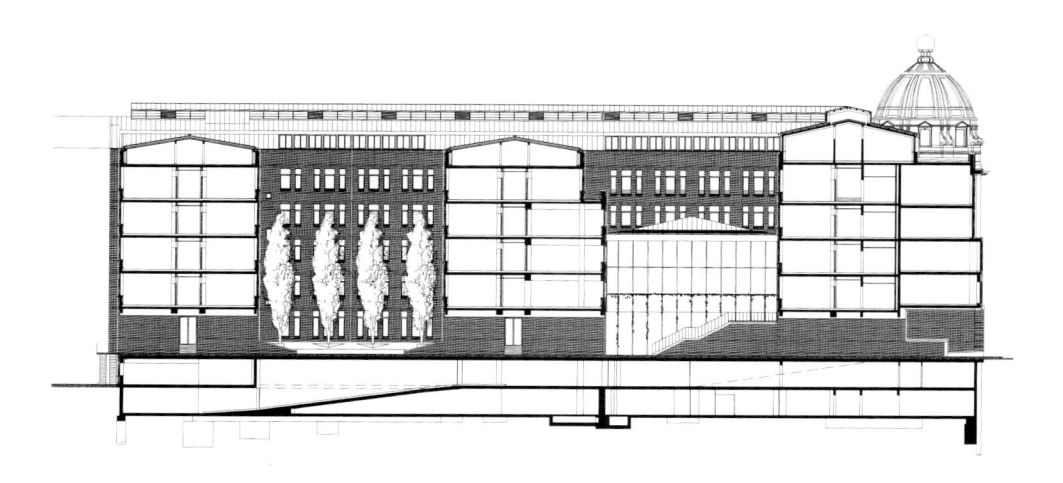

Schnitt – M 1:750

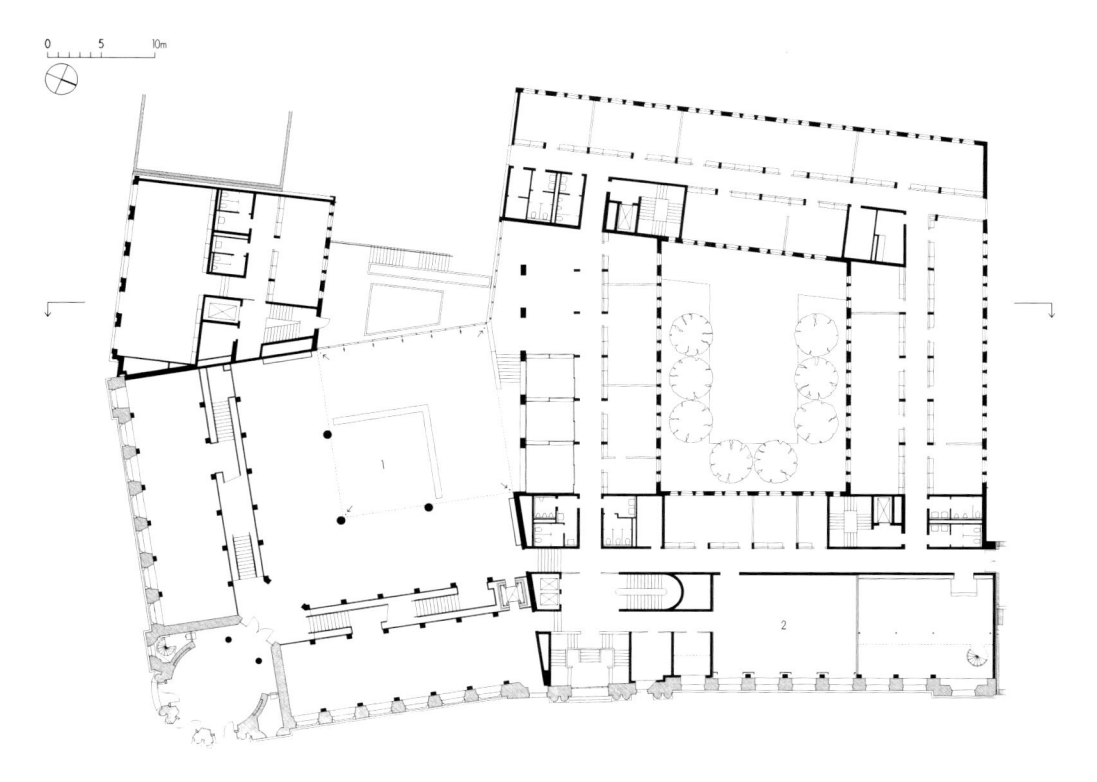

2. Erdgeschoß – M 1:750

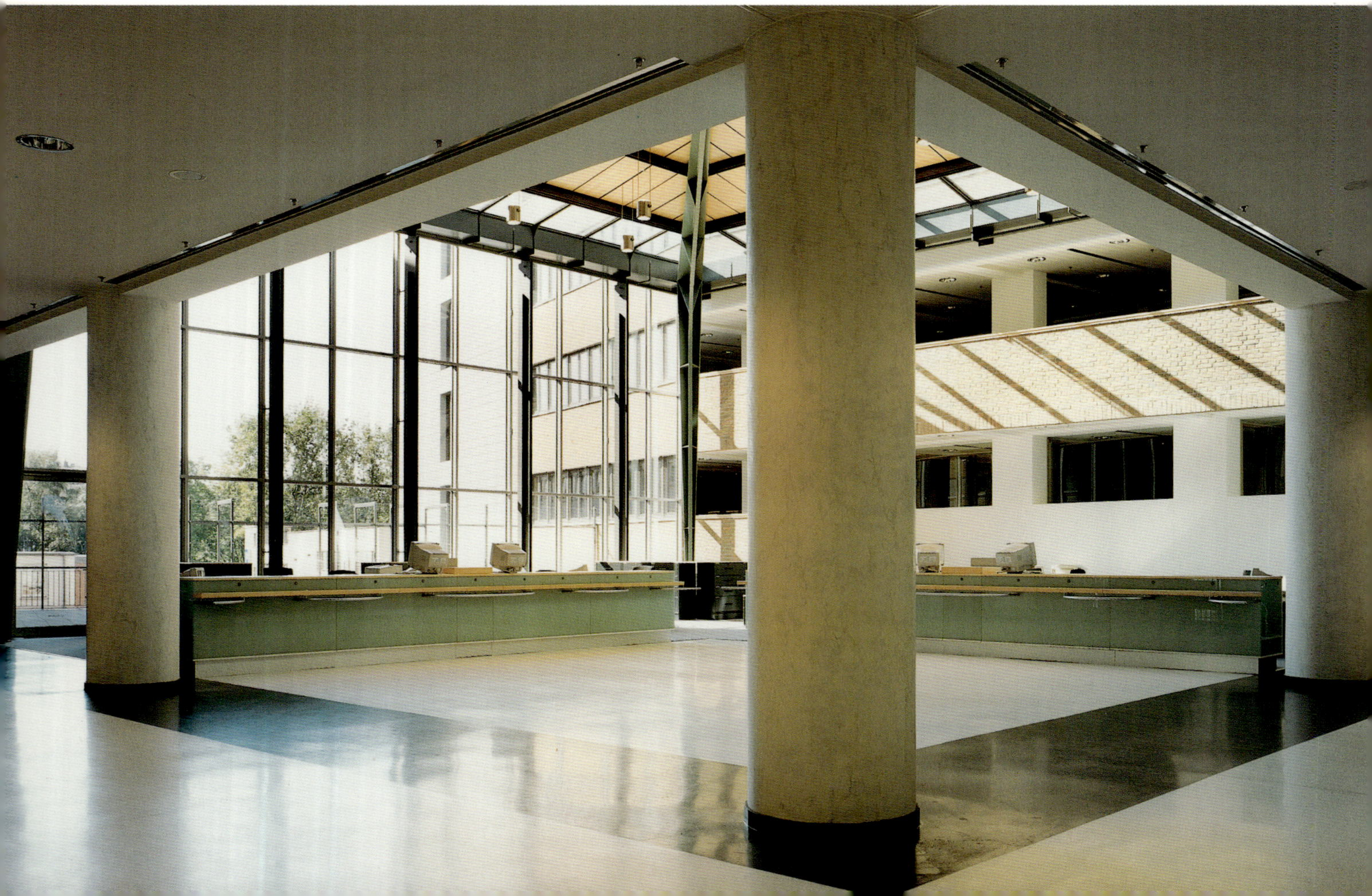

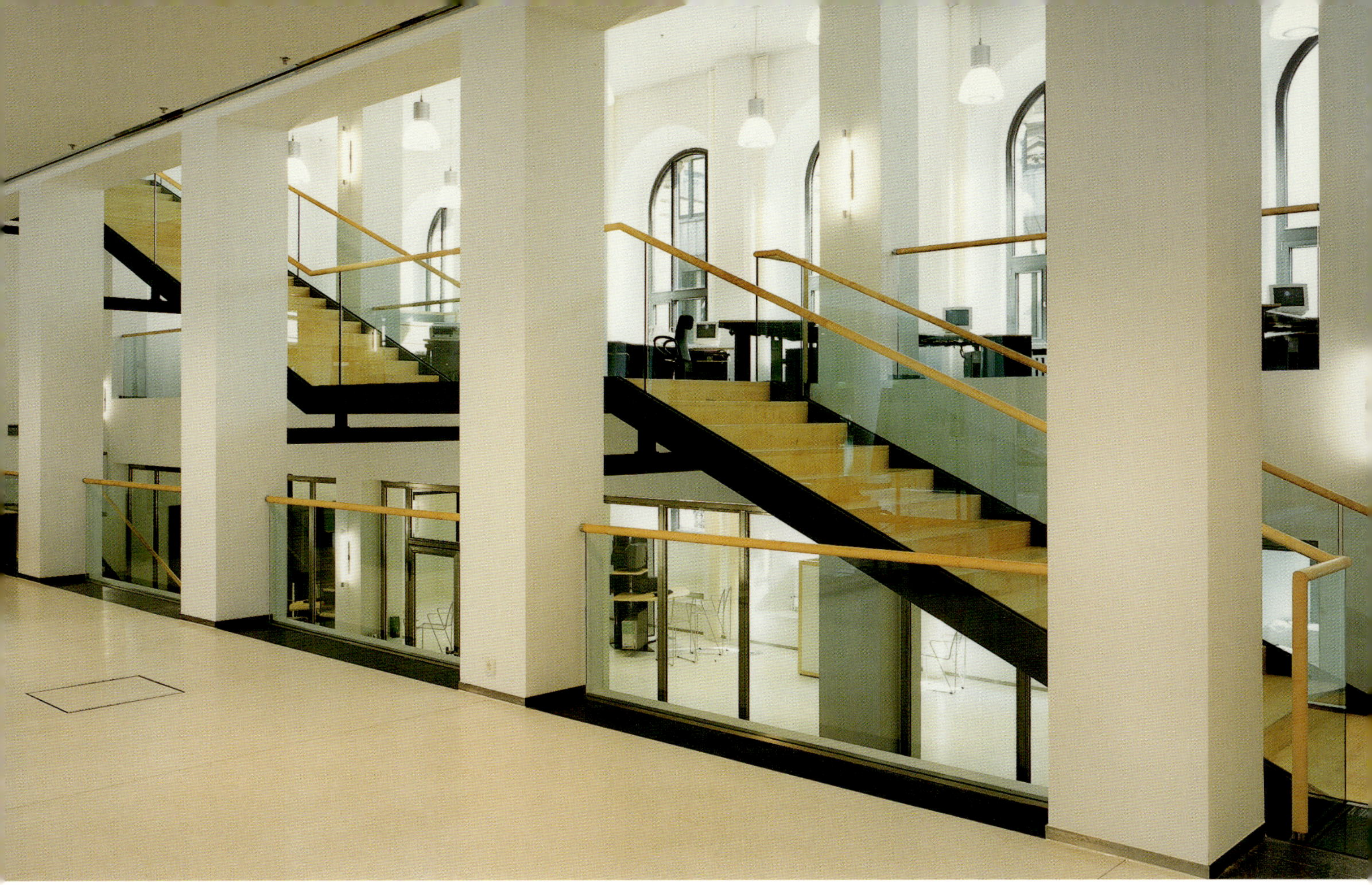

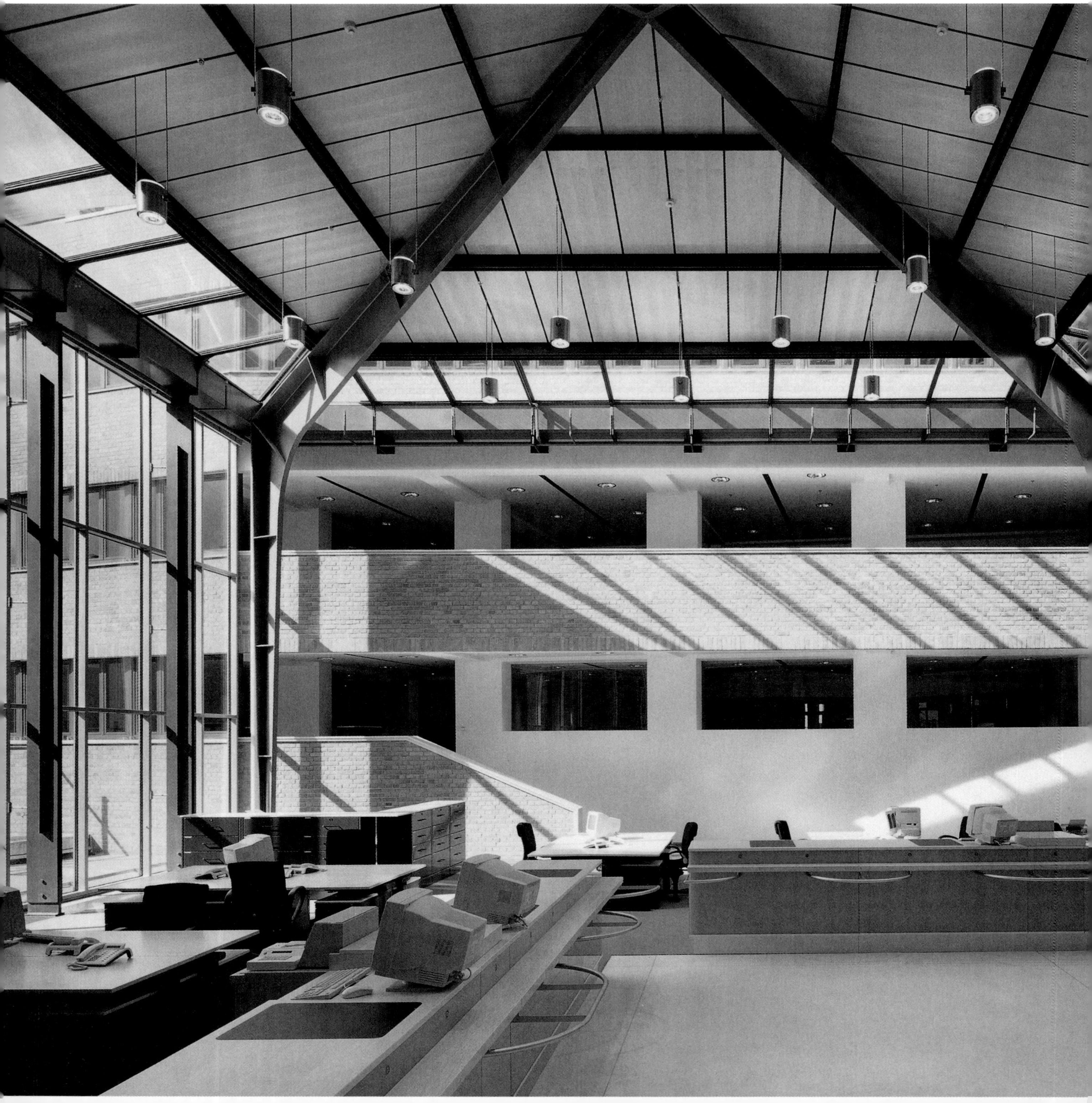

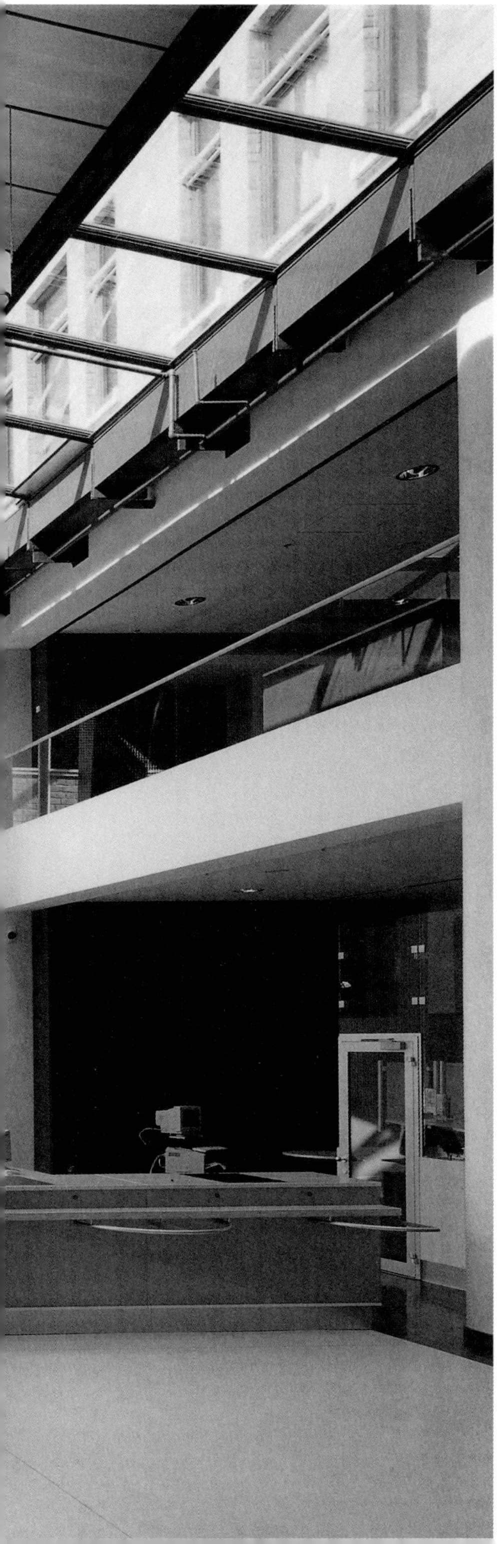

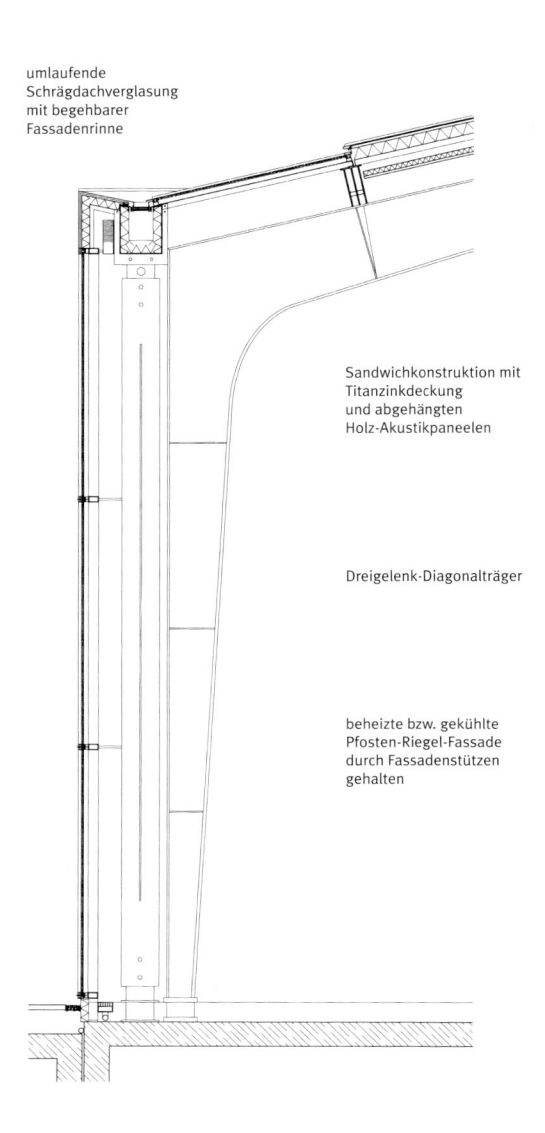

umlaufende
Schrägdachverglasung
mit begehbarer
Fassadenrinne

Sandwichkonstruktion mit
Titanzinkdeckung
und abgehängten
Holz-Akustikpaneelen

Dreigelenk-Diagonalträger

beheizte bzw. gekühlte
Pfosten-Riegel-Fassade
durch Fassadenstützen
gehalten

Detail Kundenhallenfassade

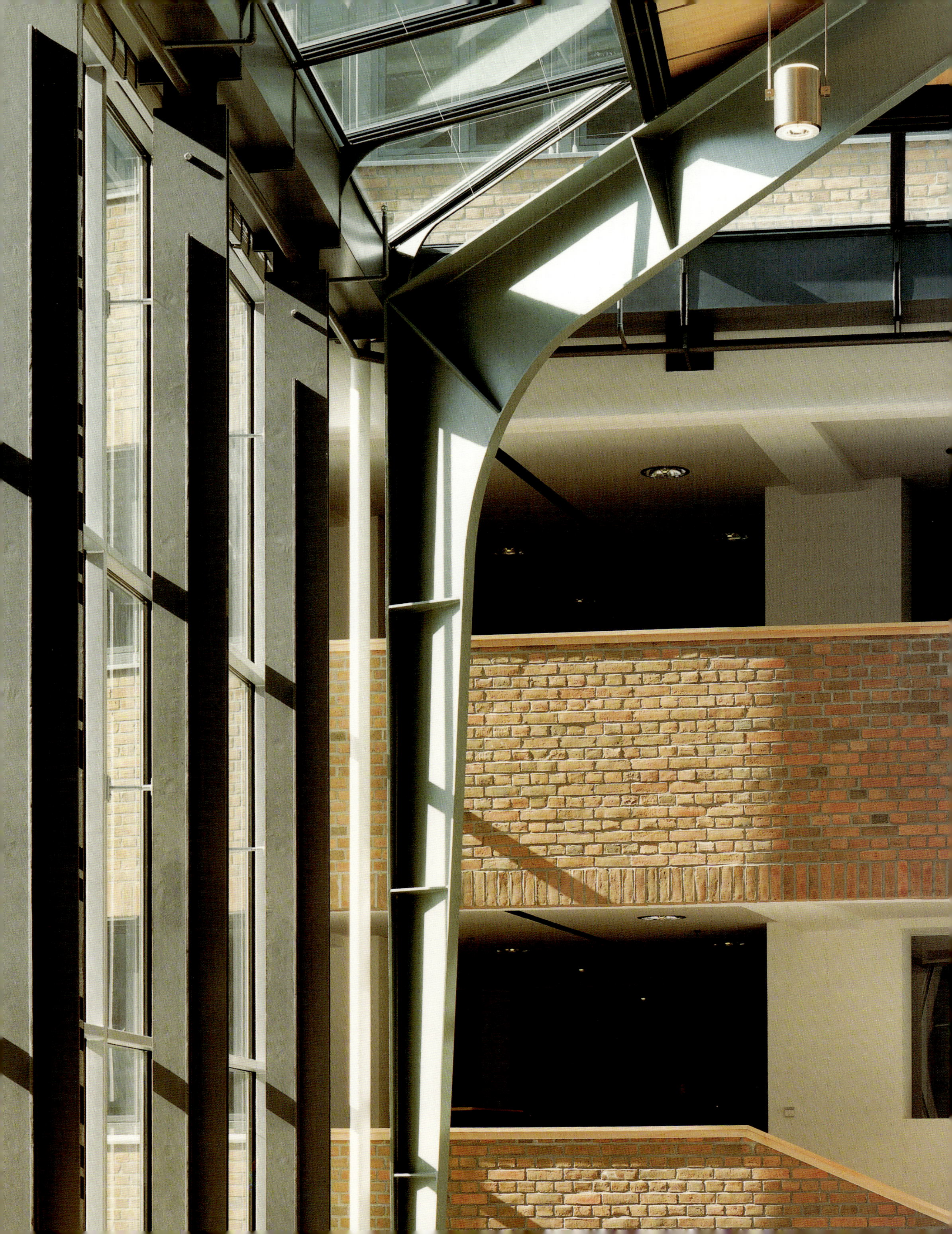

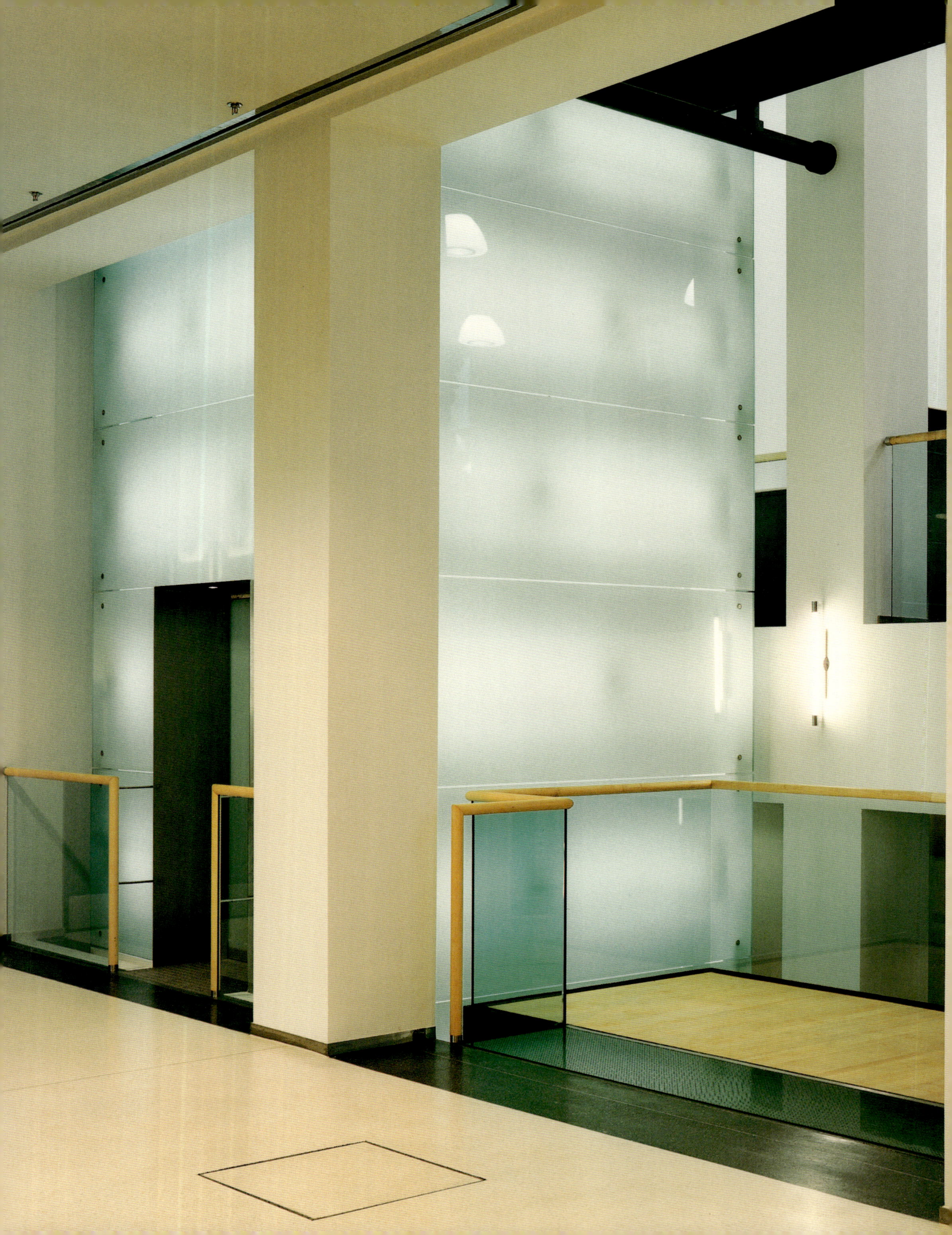

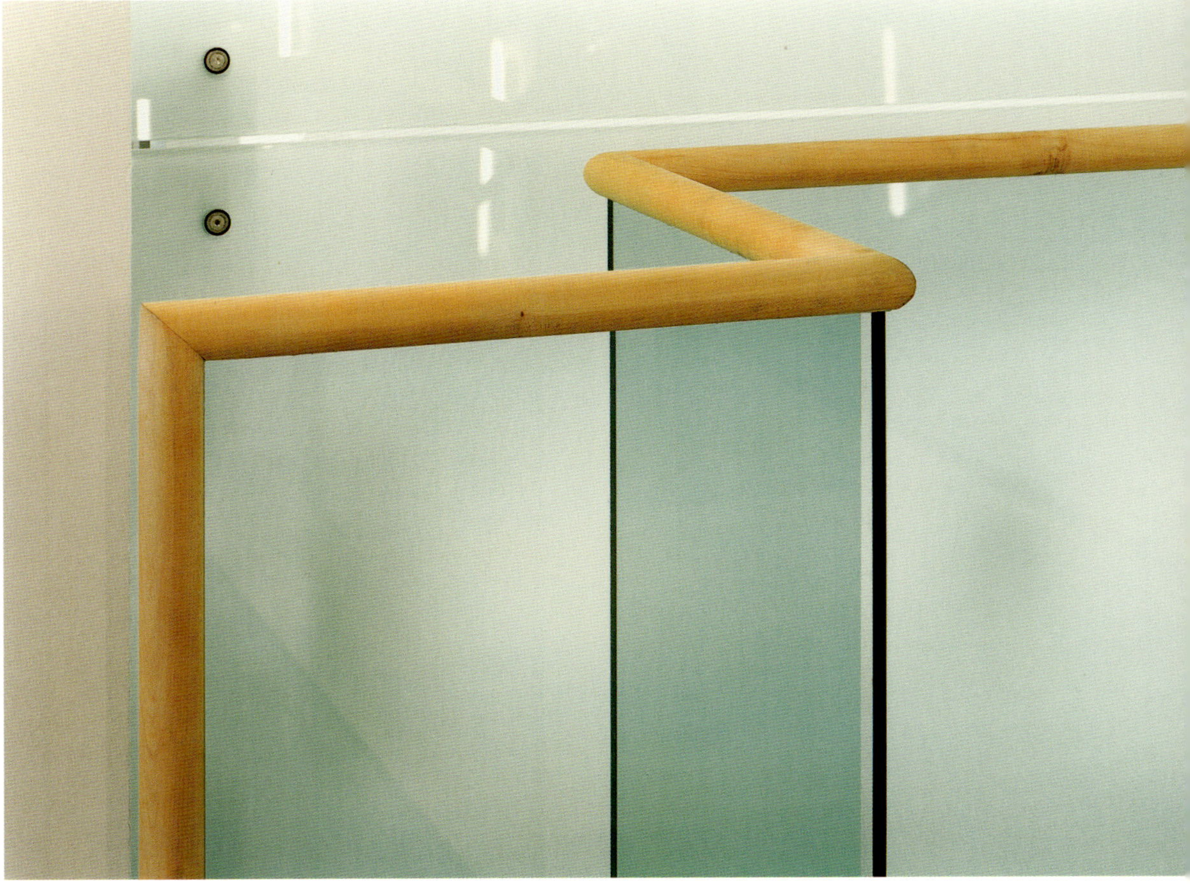

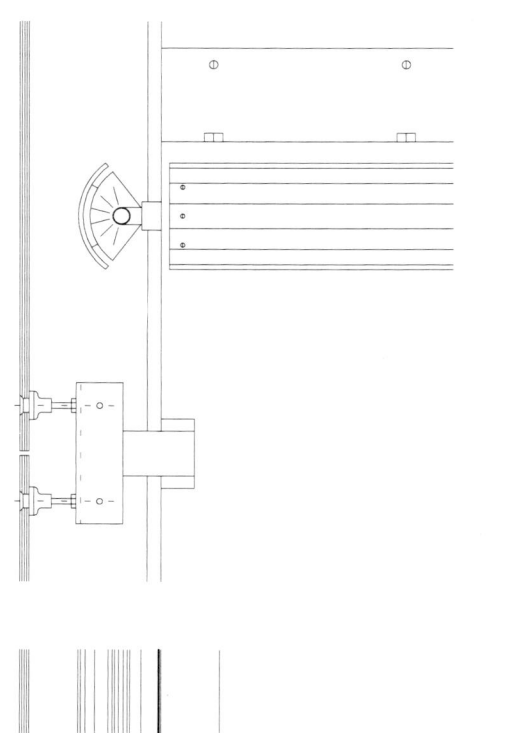

Revisionsklappe
Beleuchtung

Leuchtstoffröhre mit
Plexiglasdiffusor

Multipoint Glashalter

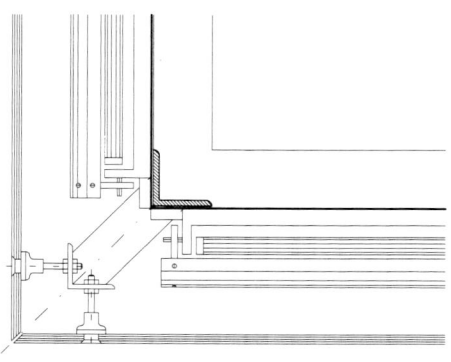

Schachtgerüst mit weiß-
lackierter Blechverkleidung

16 mm VSG
transluzent

Detail Glasaufzug

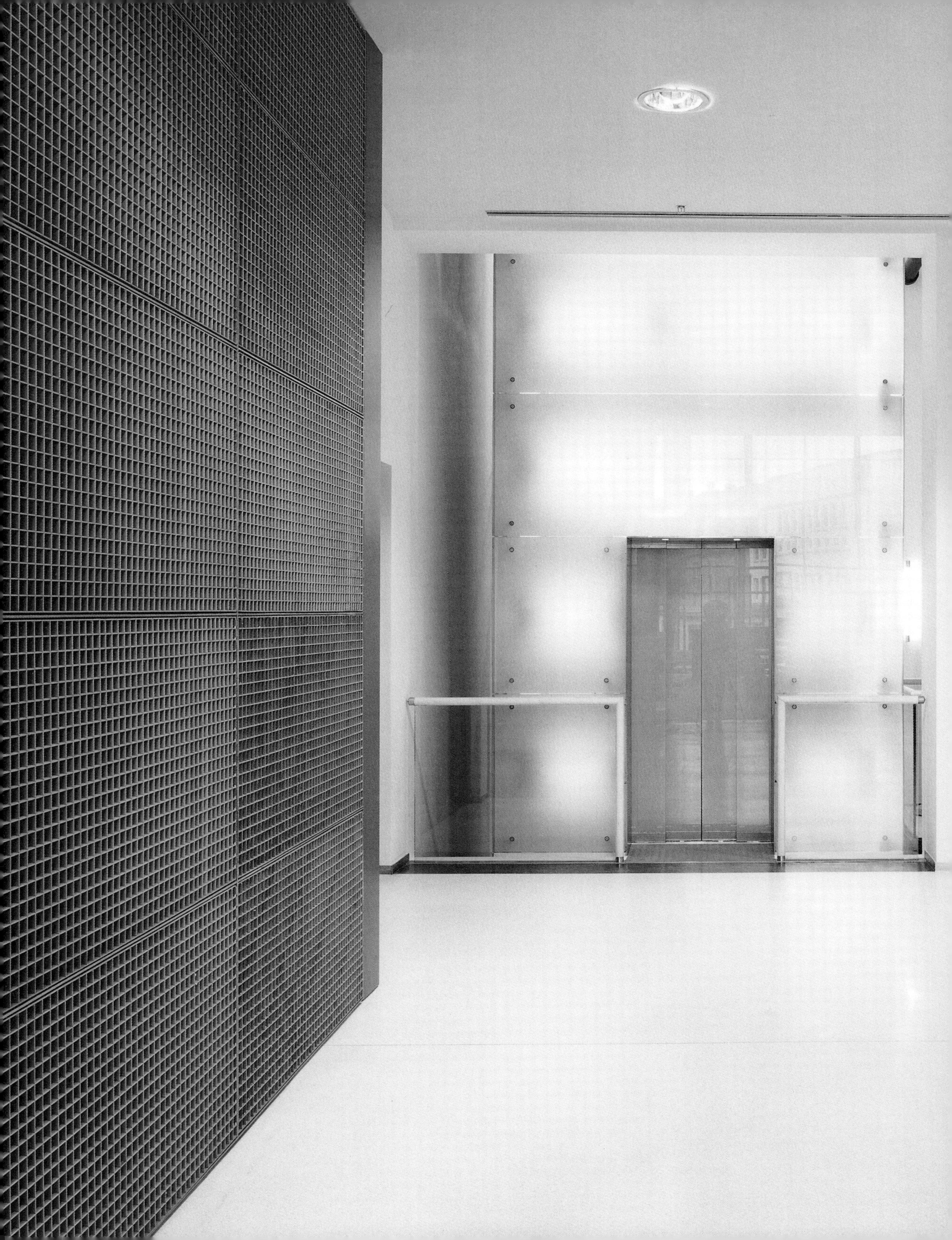

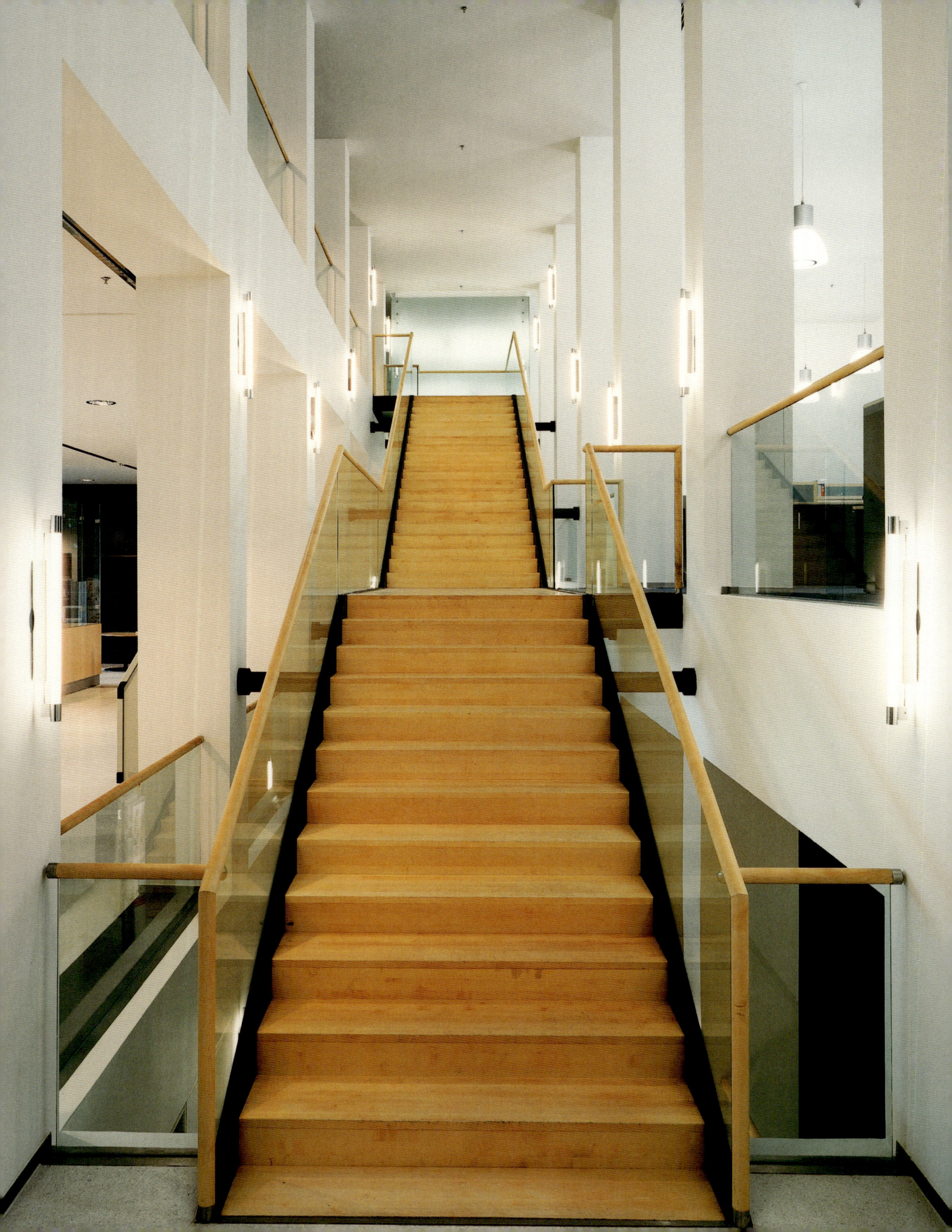

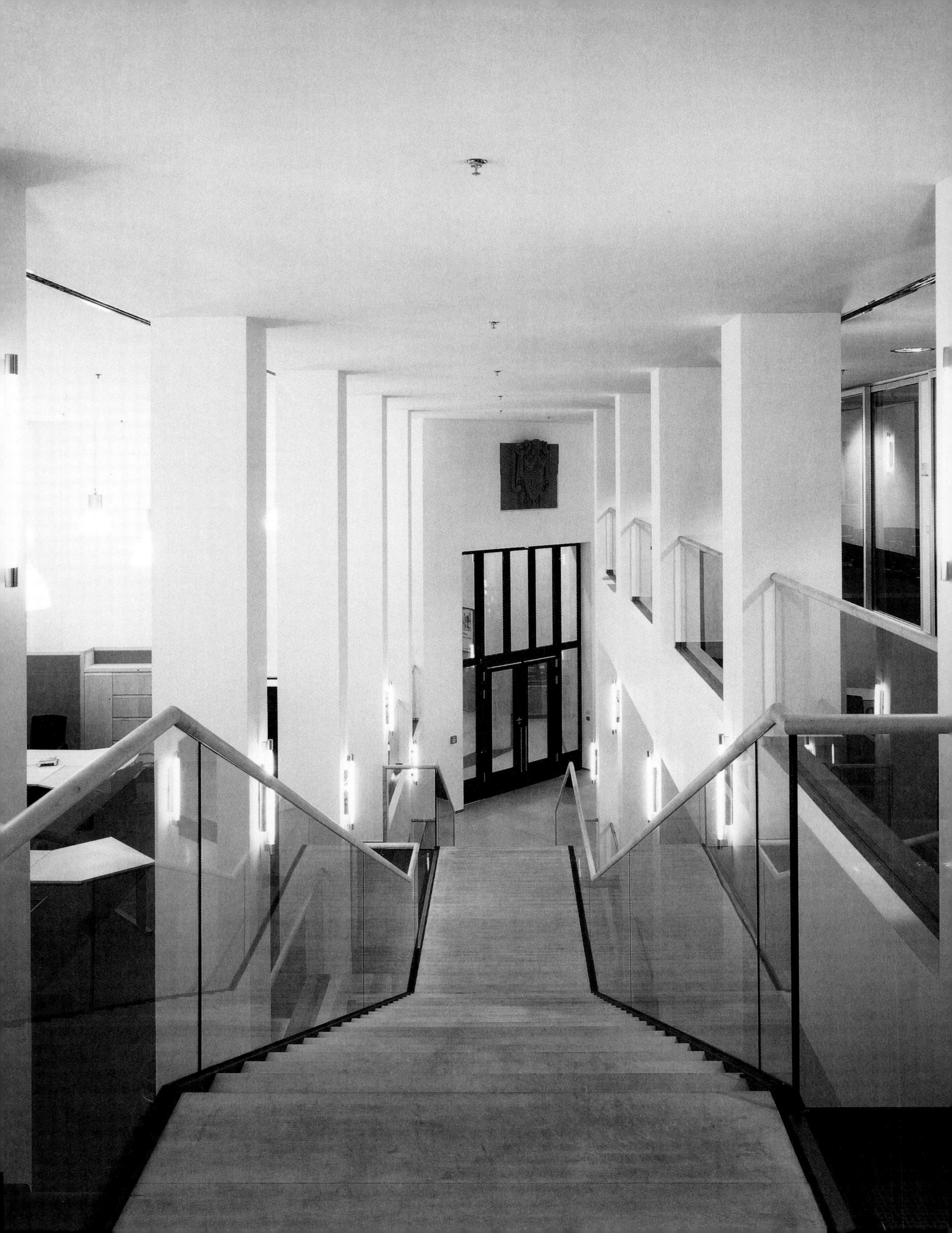

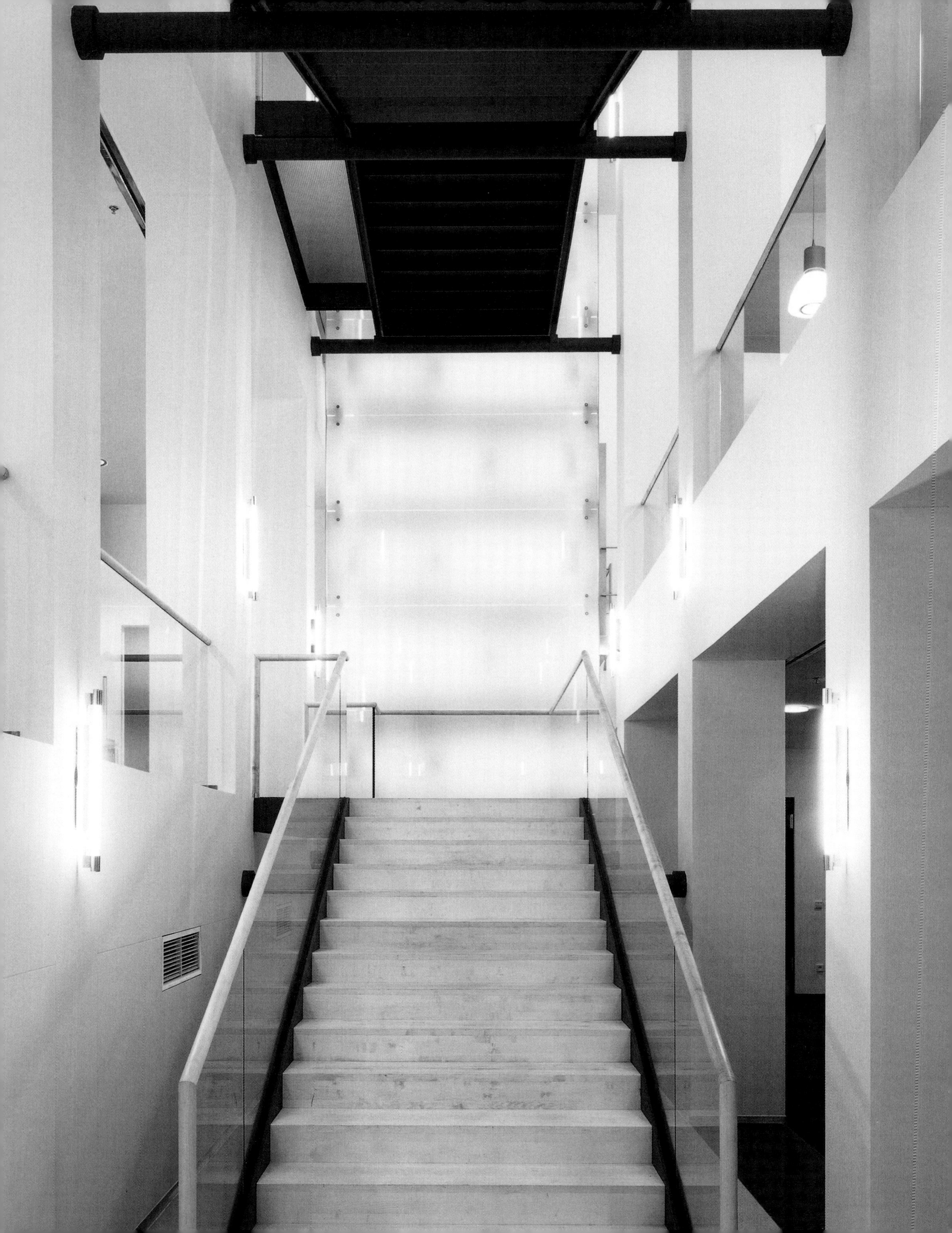

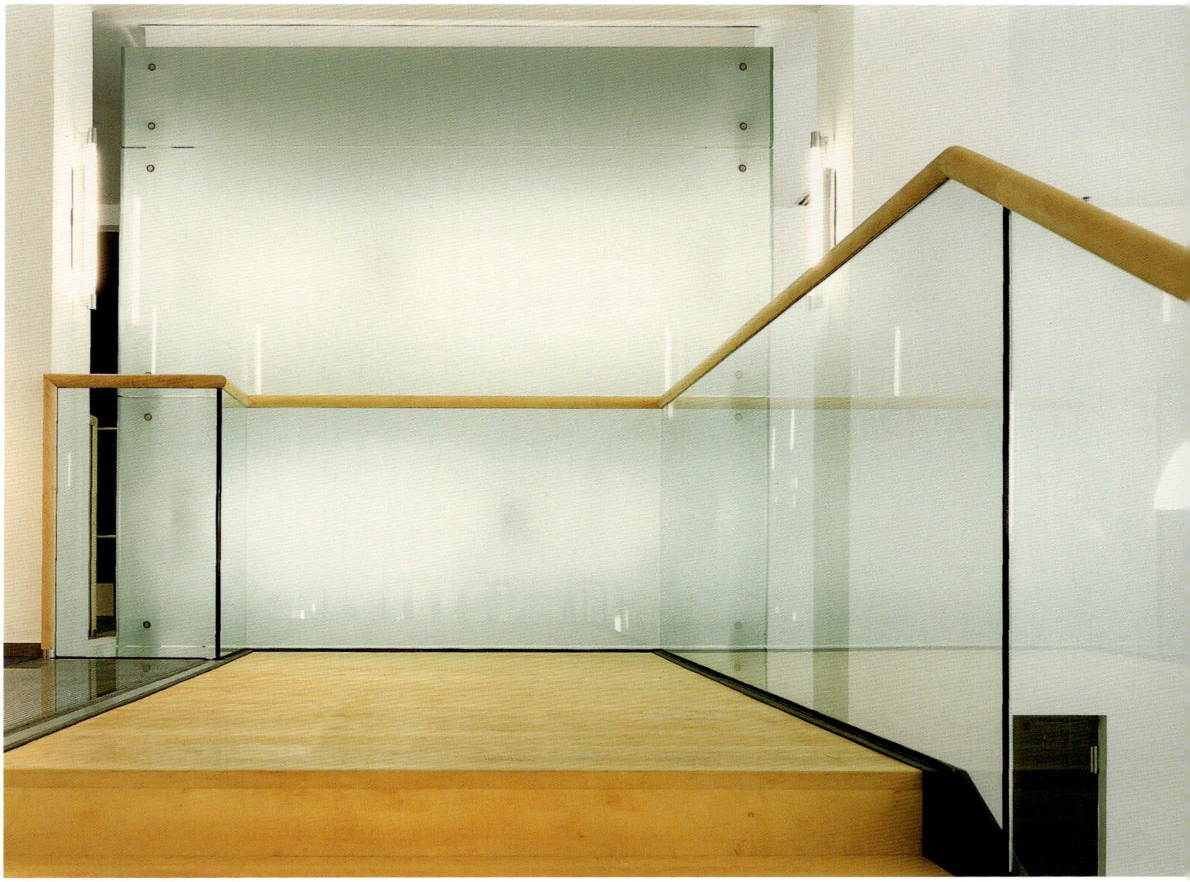

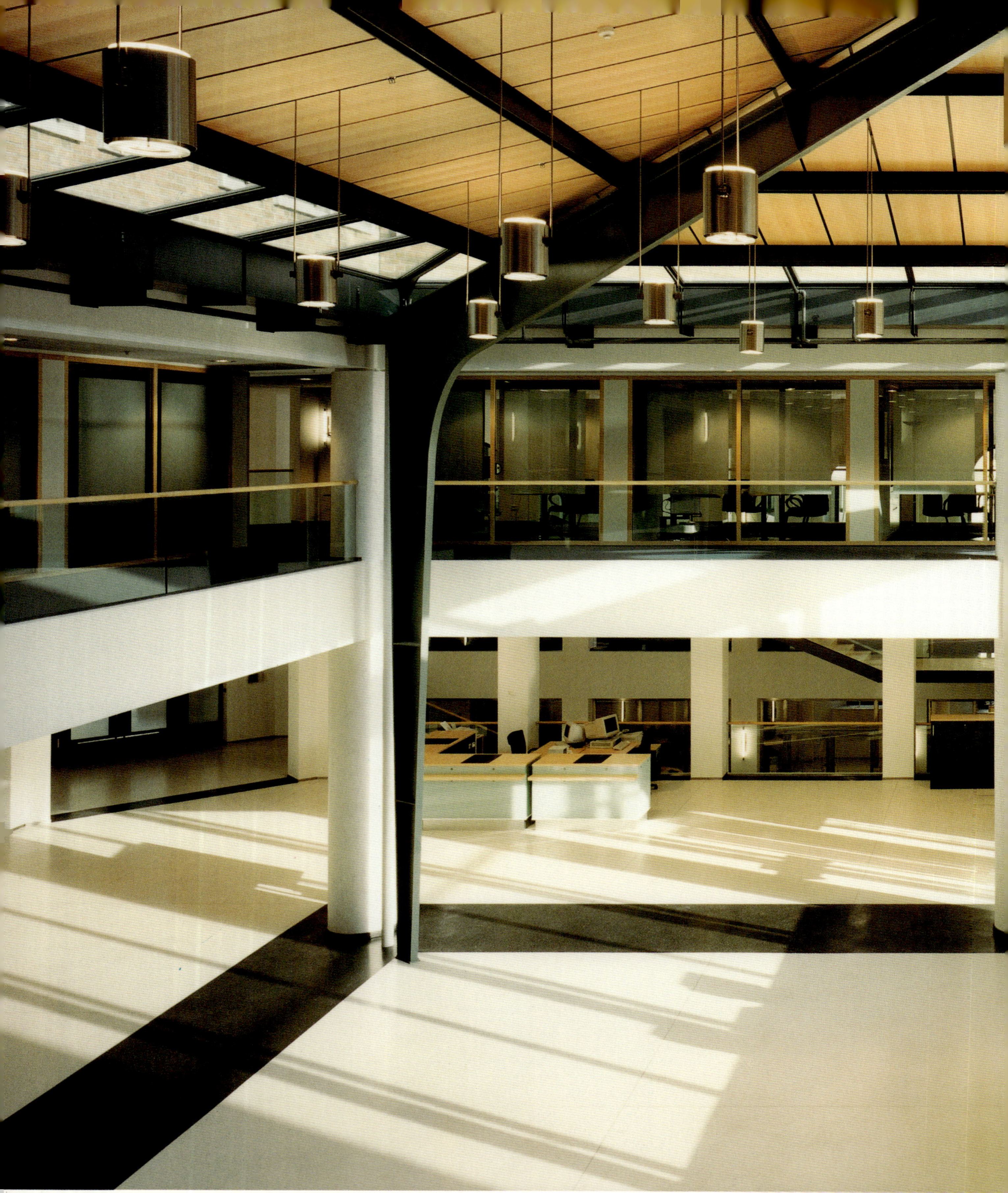

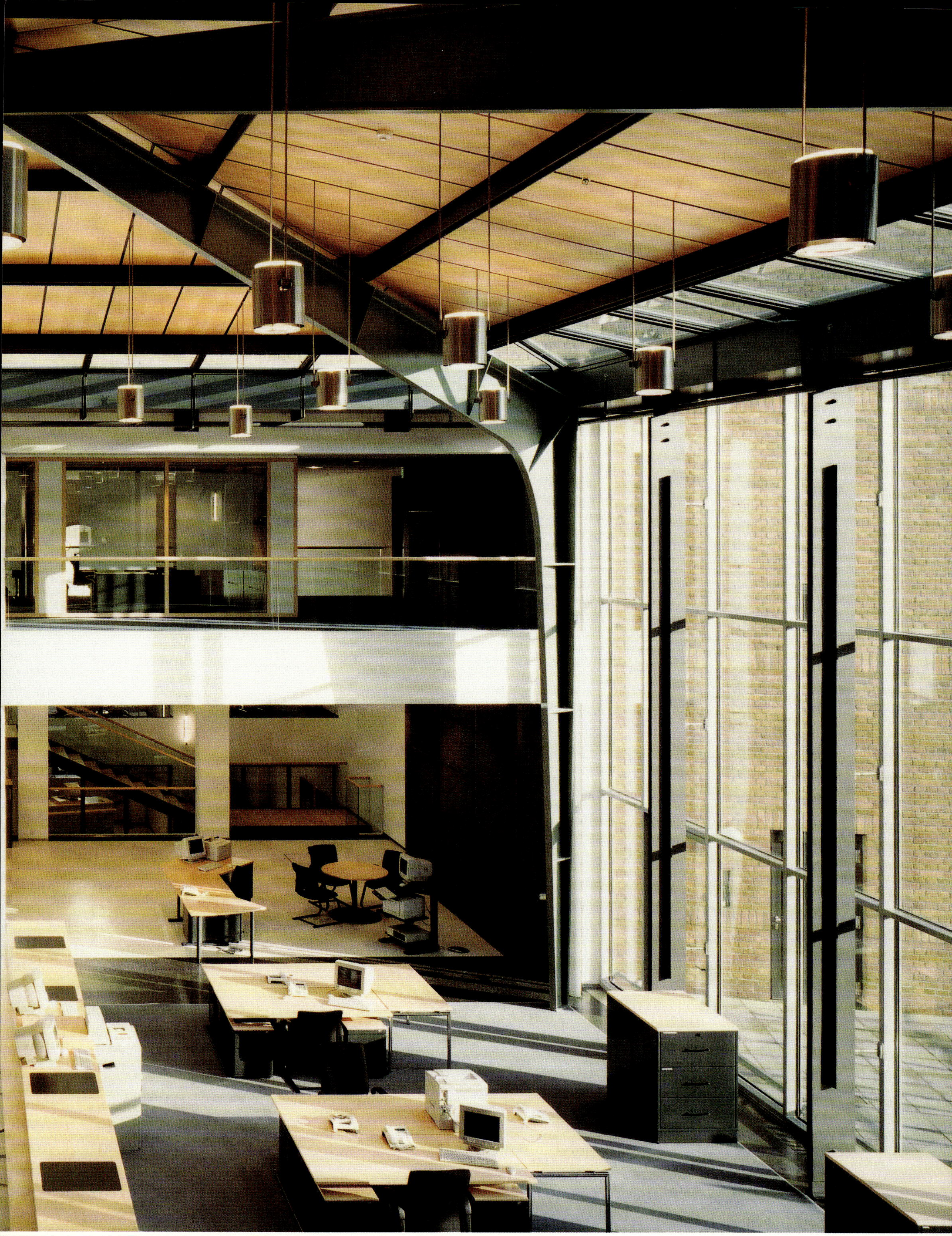

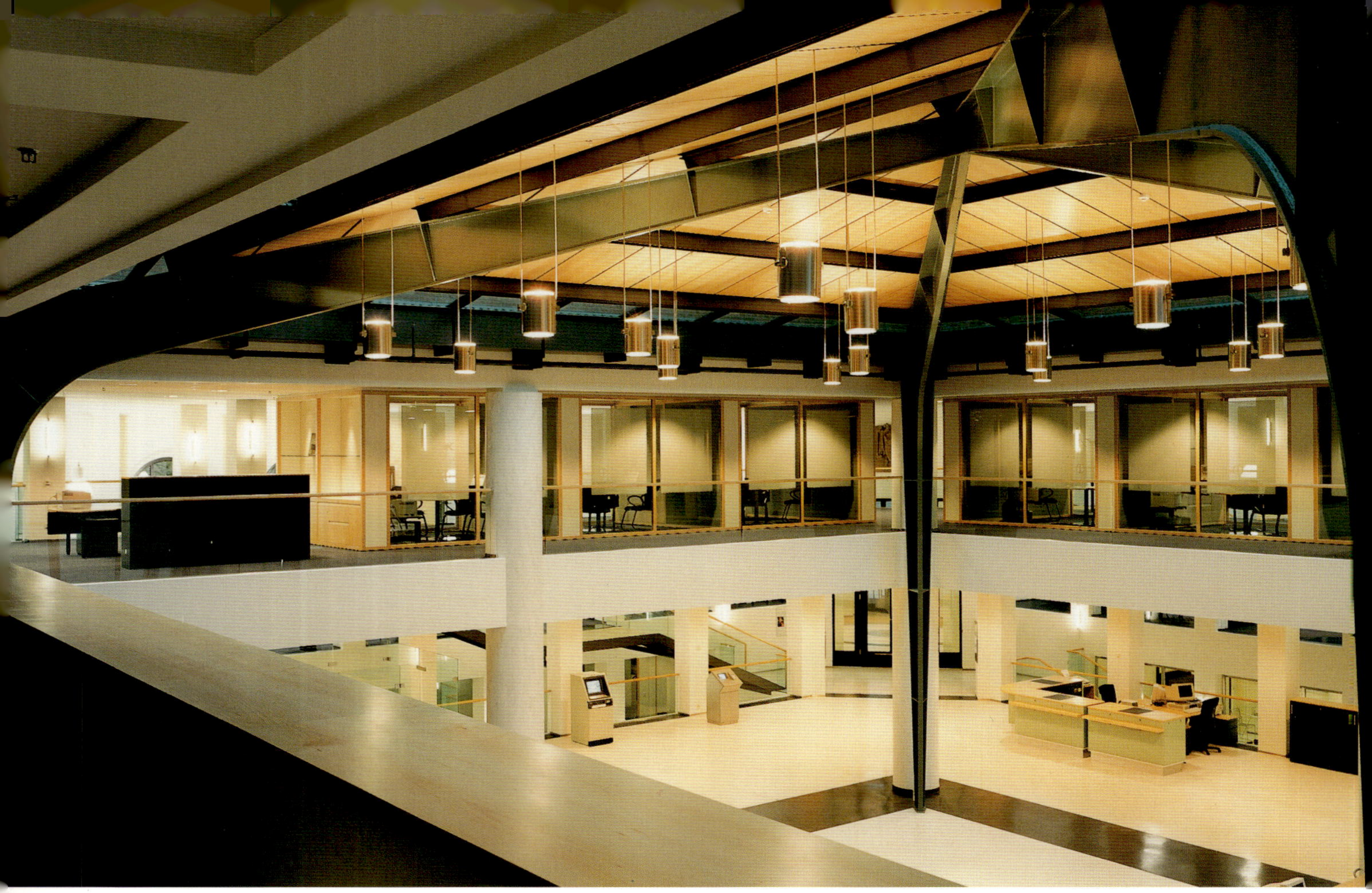

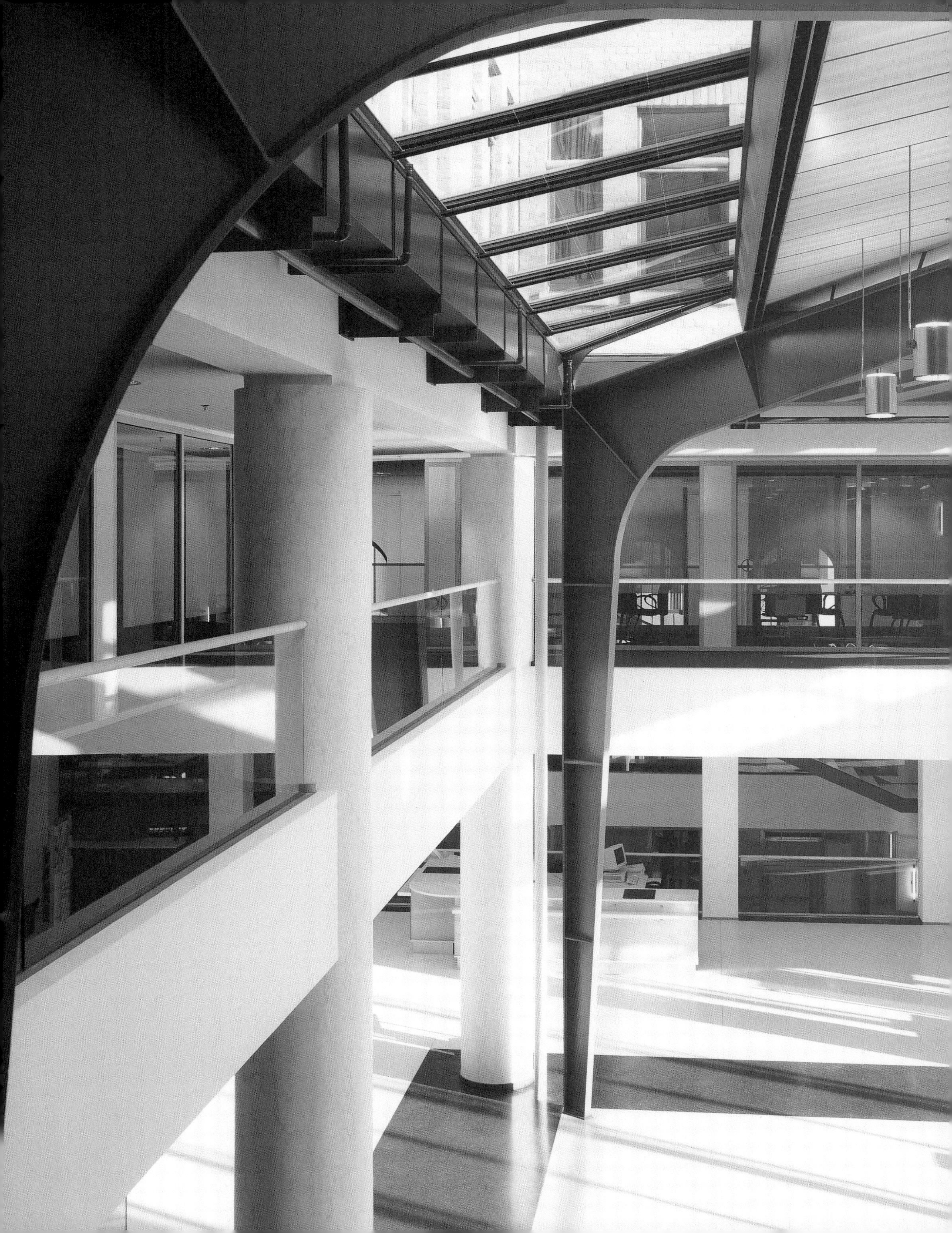

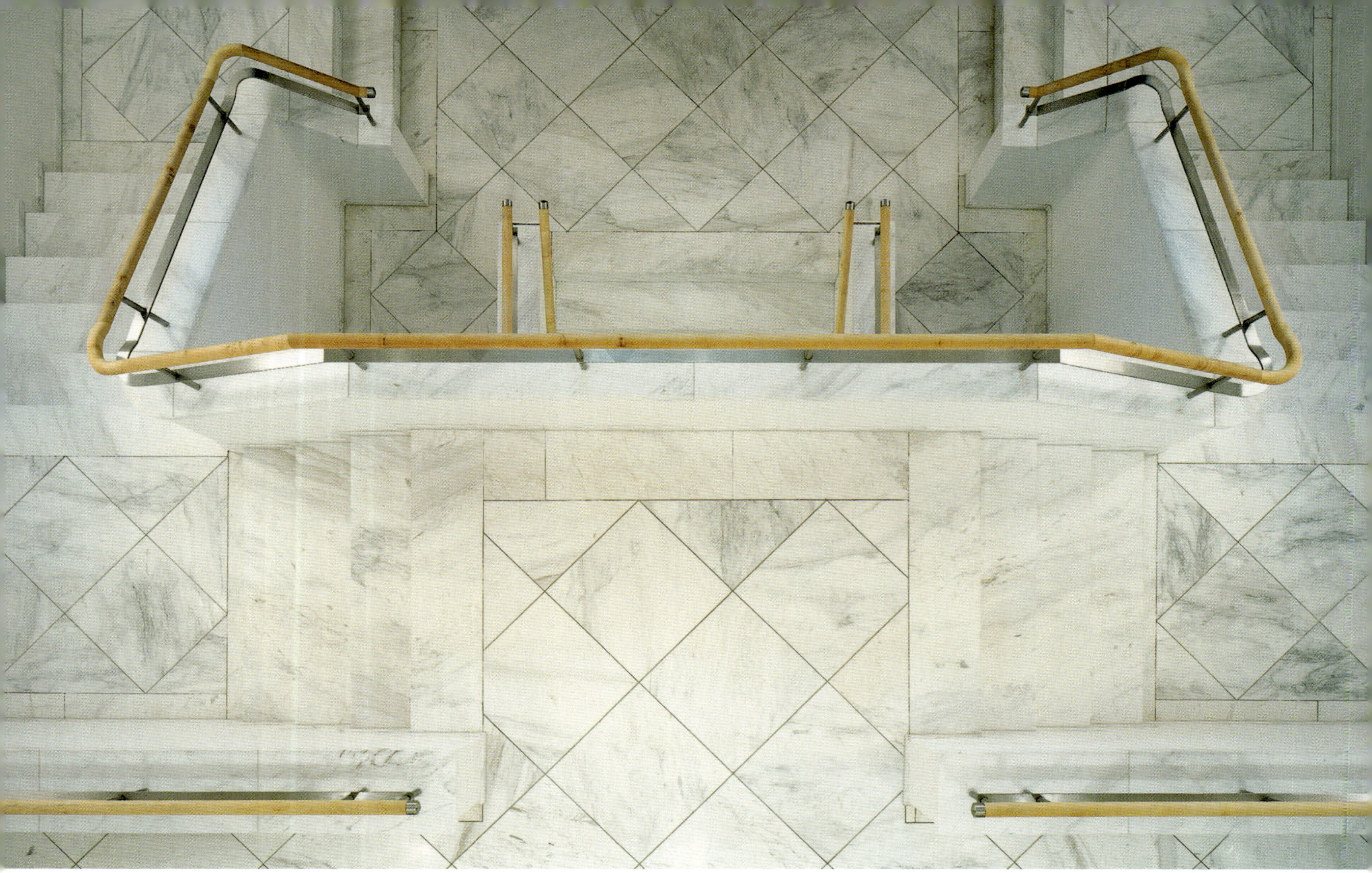

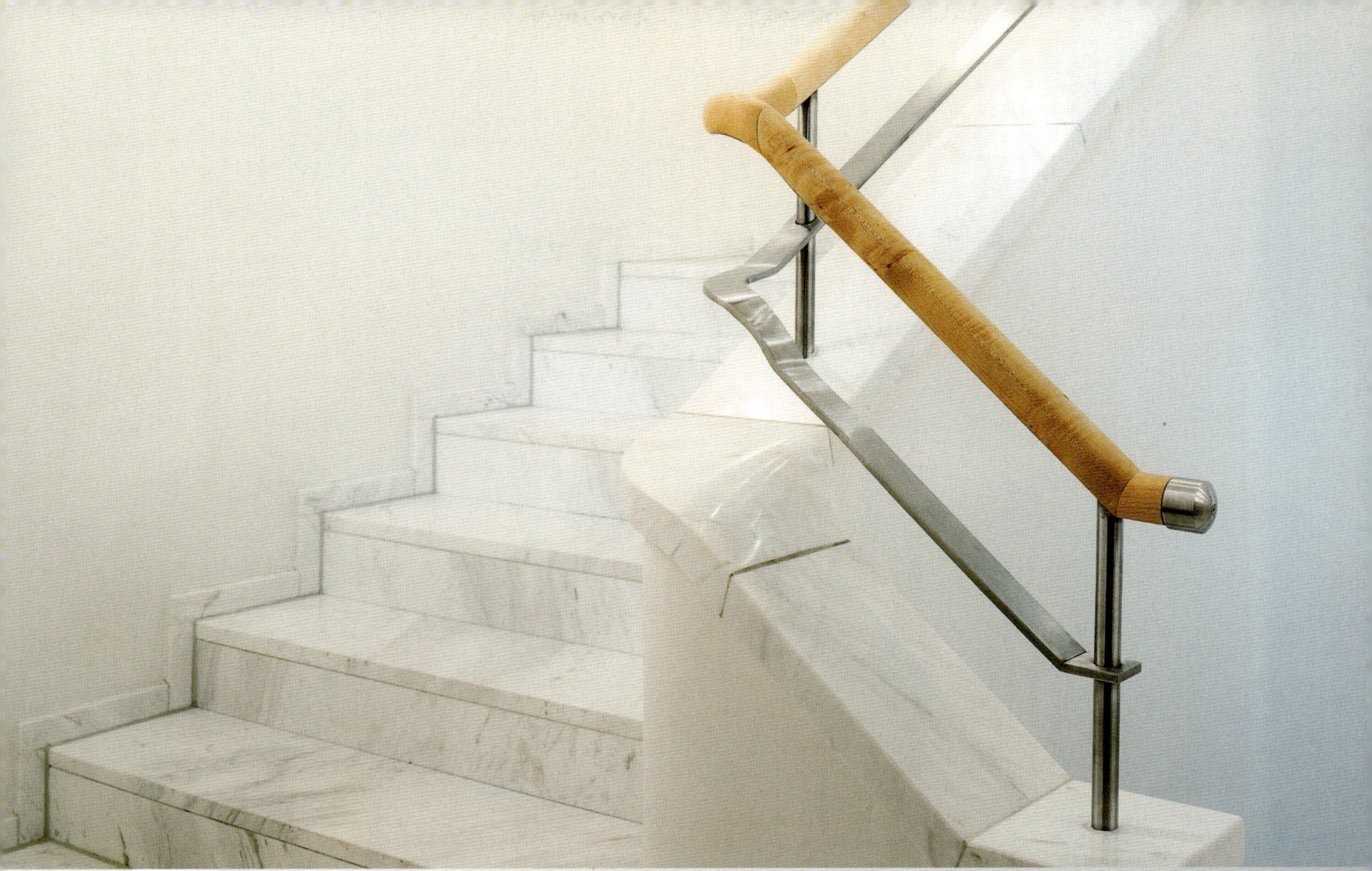

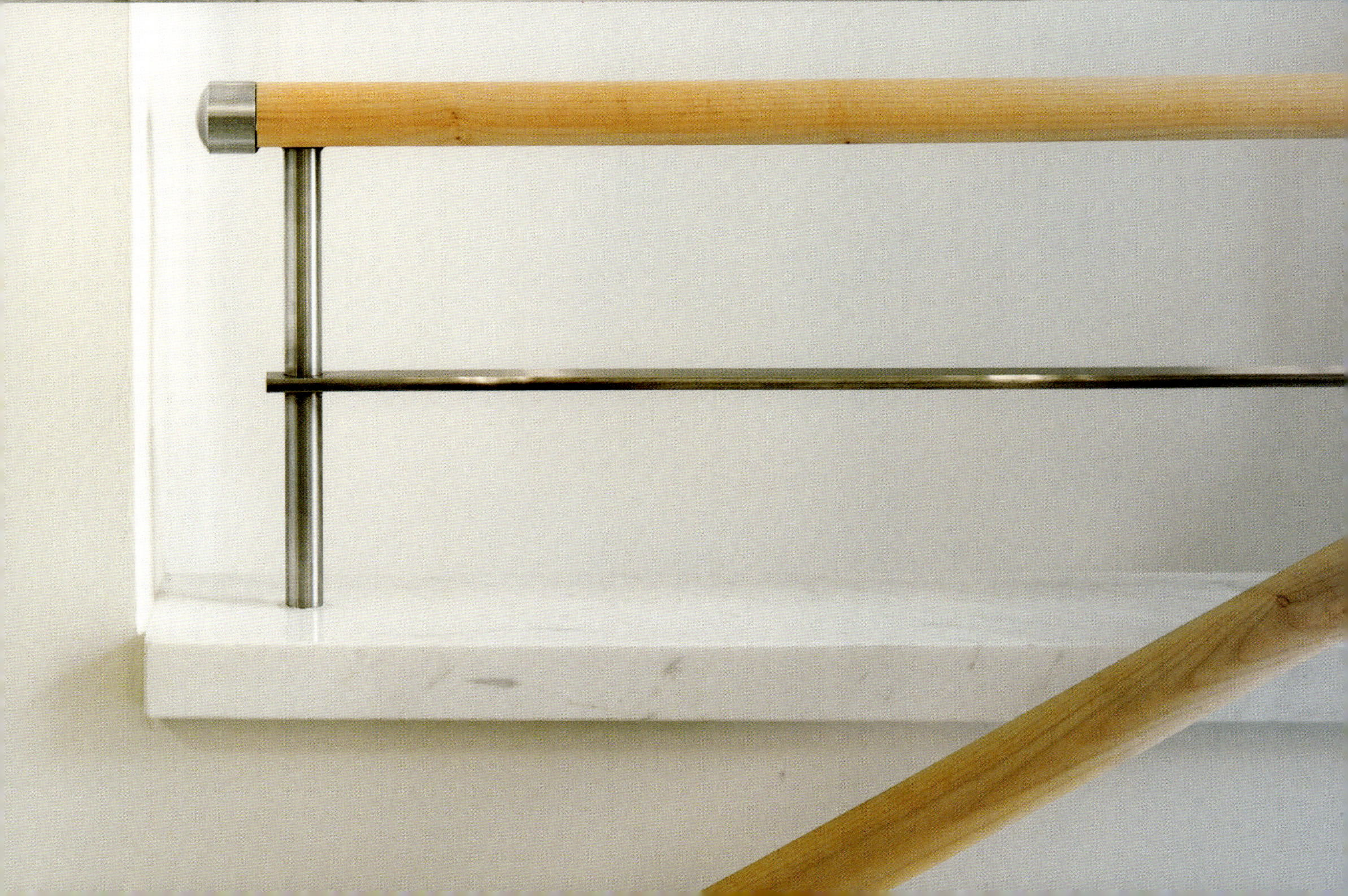

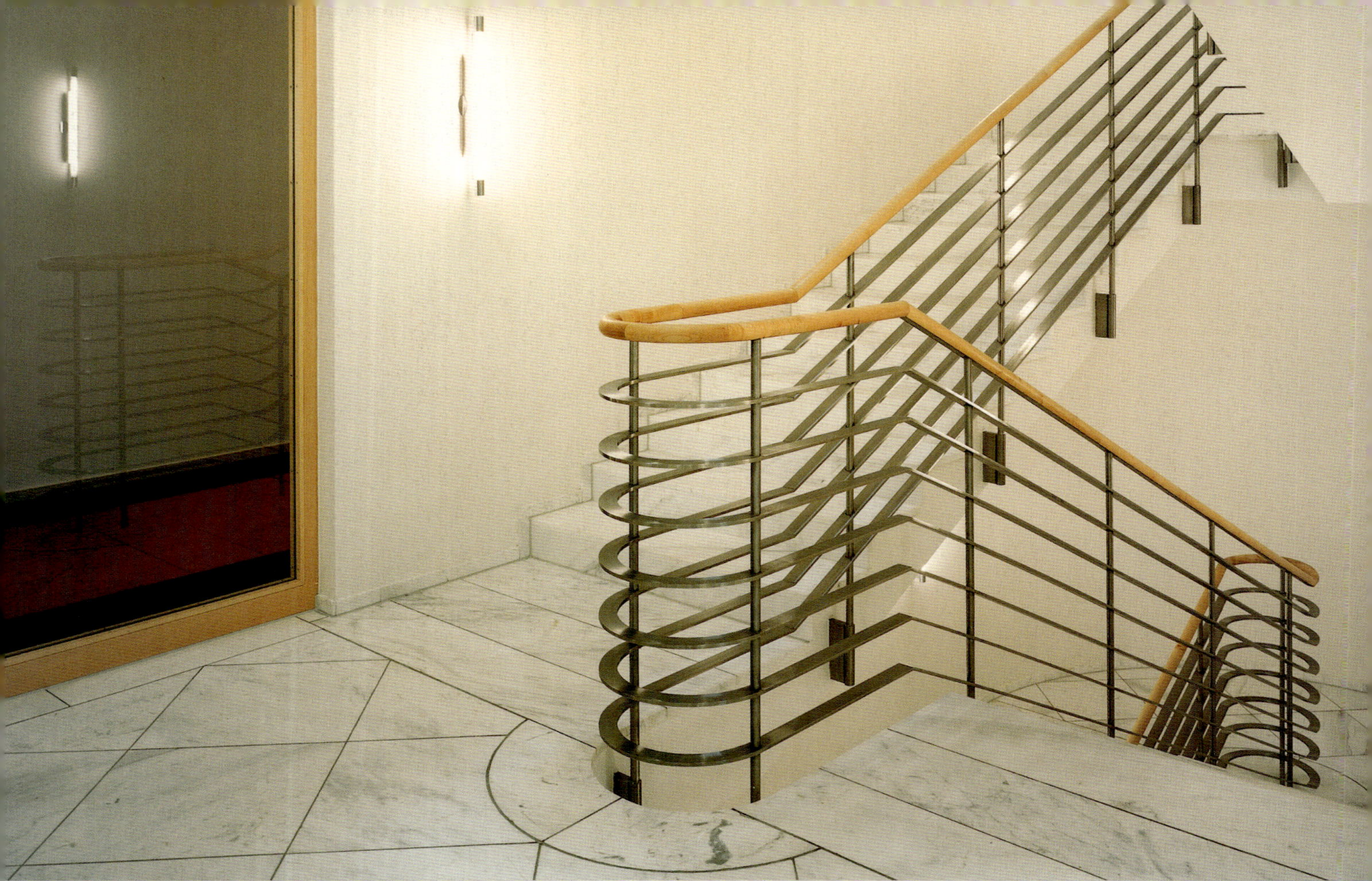

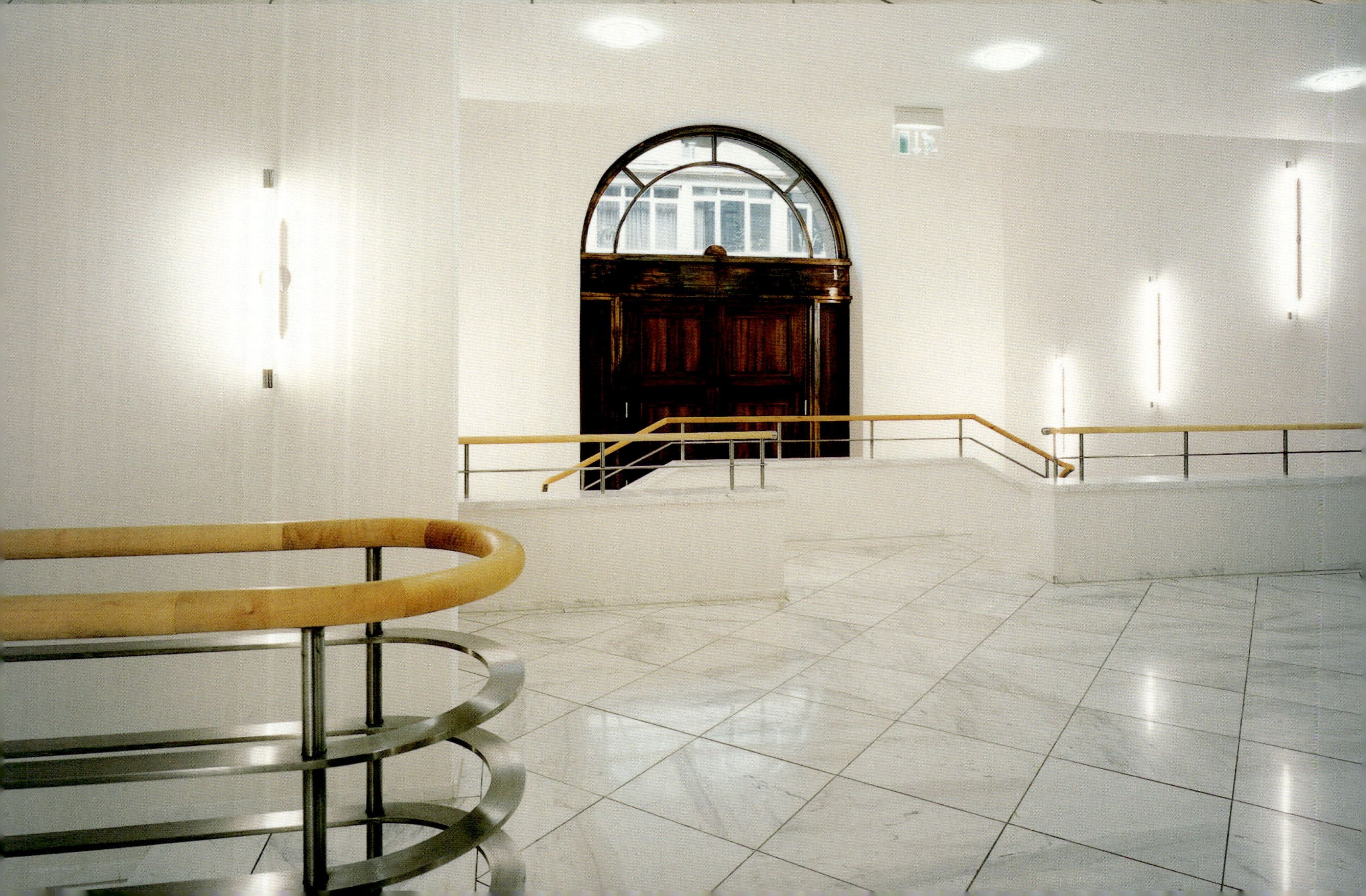

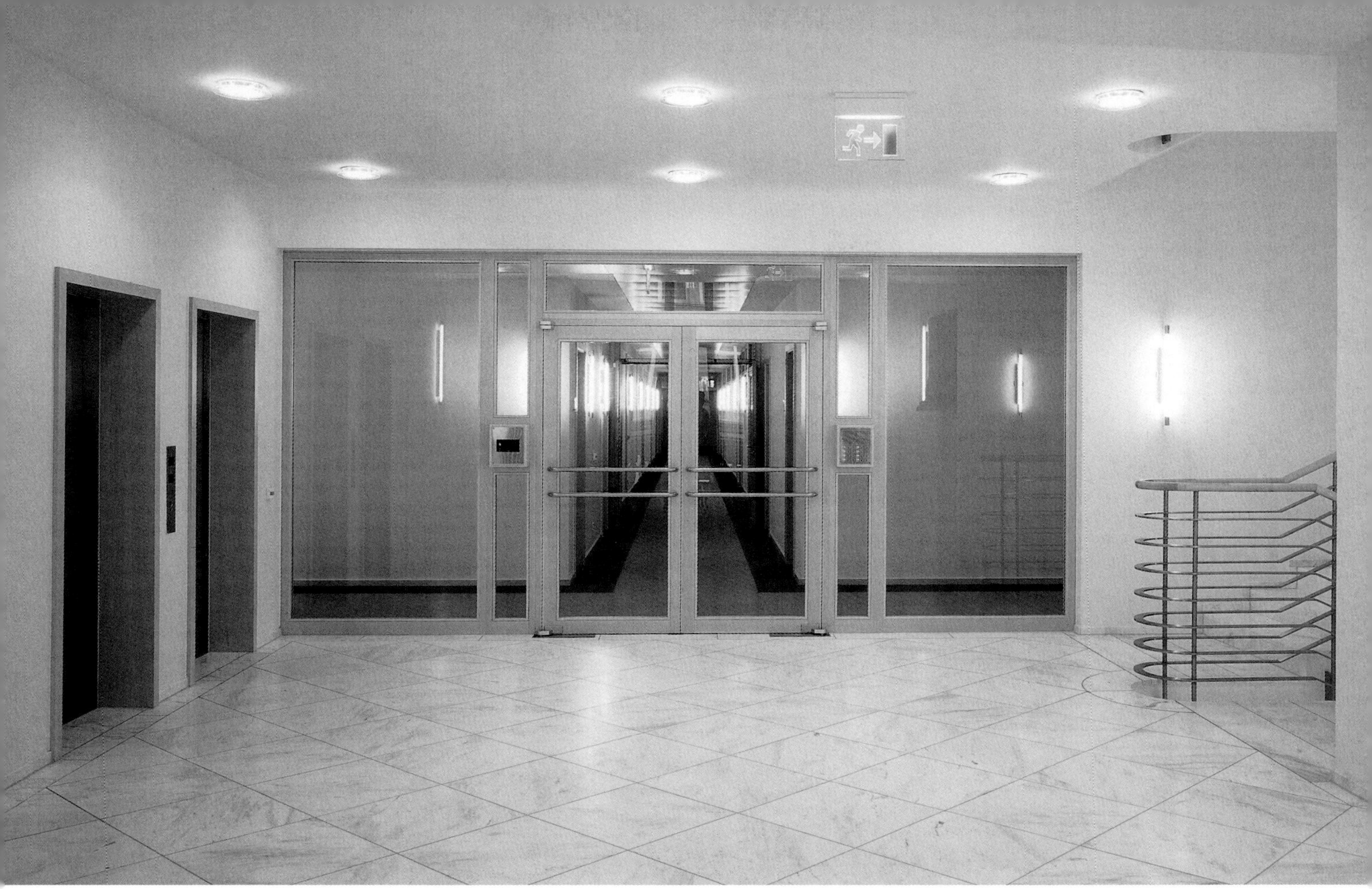

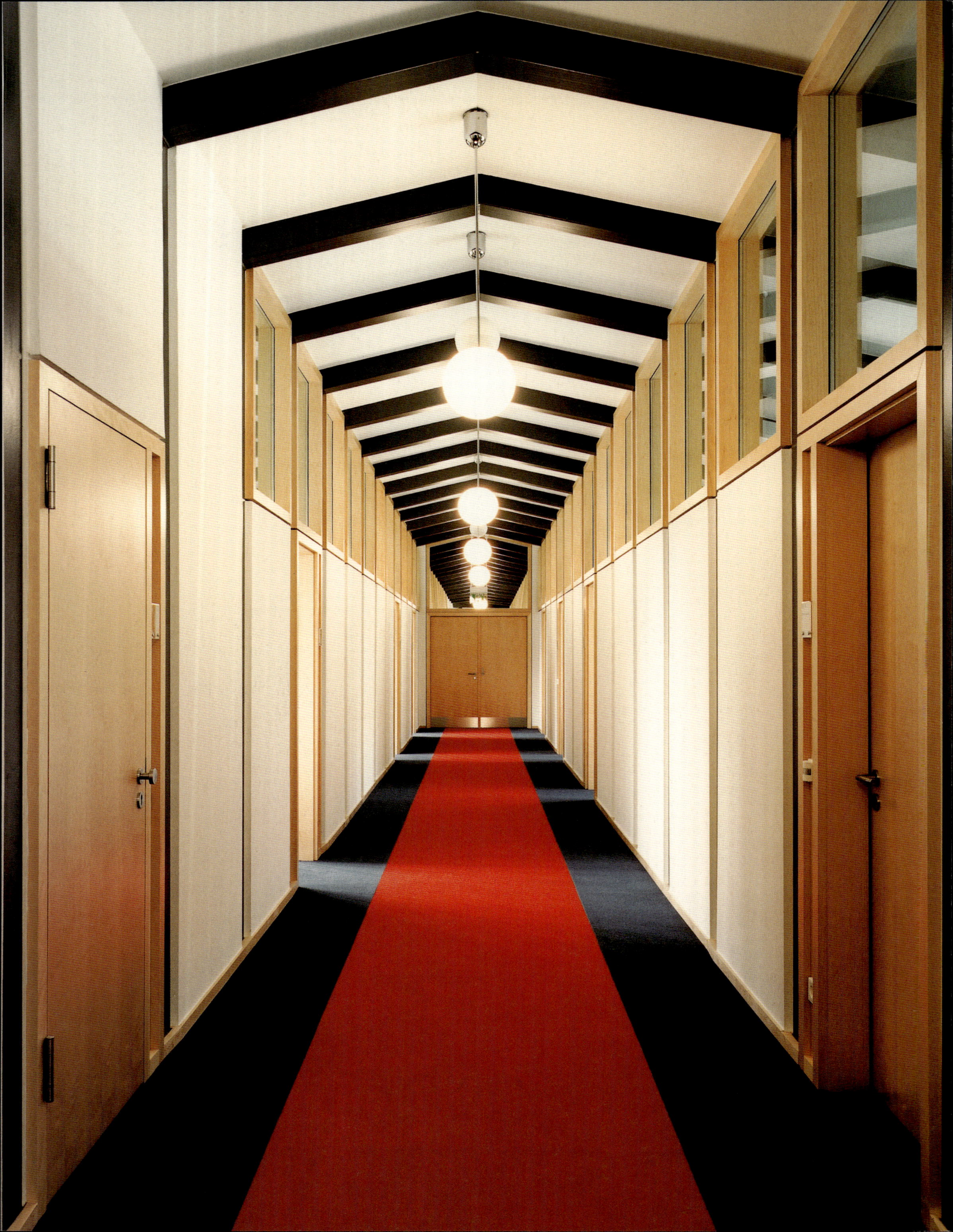

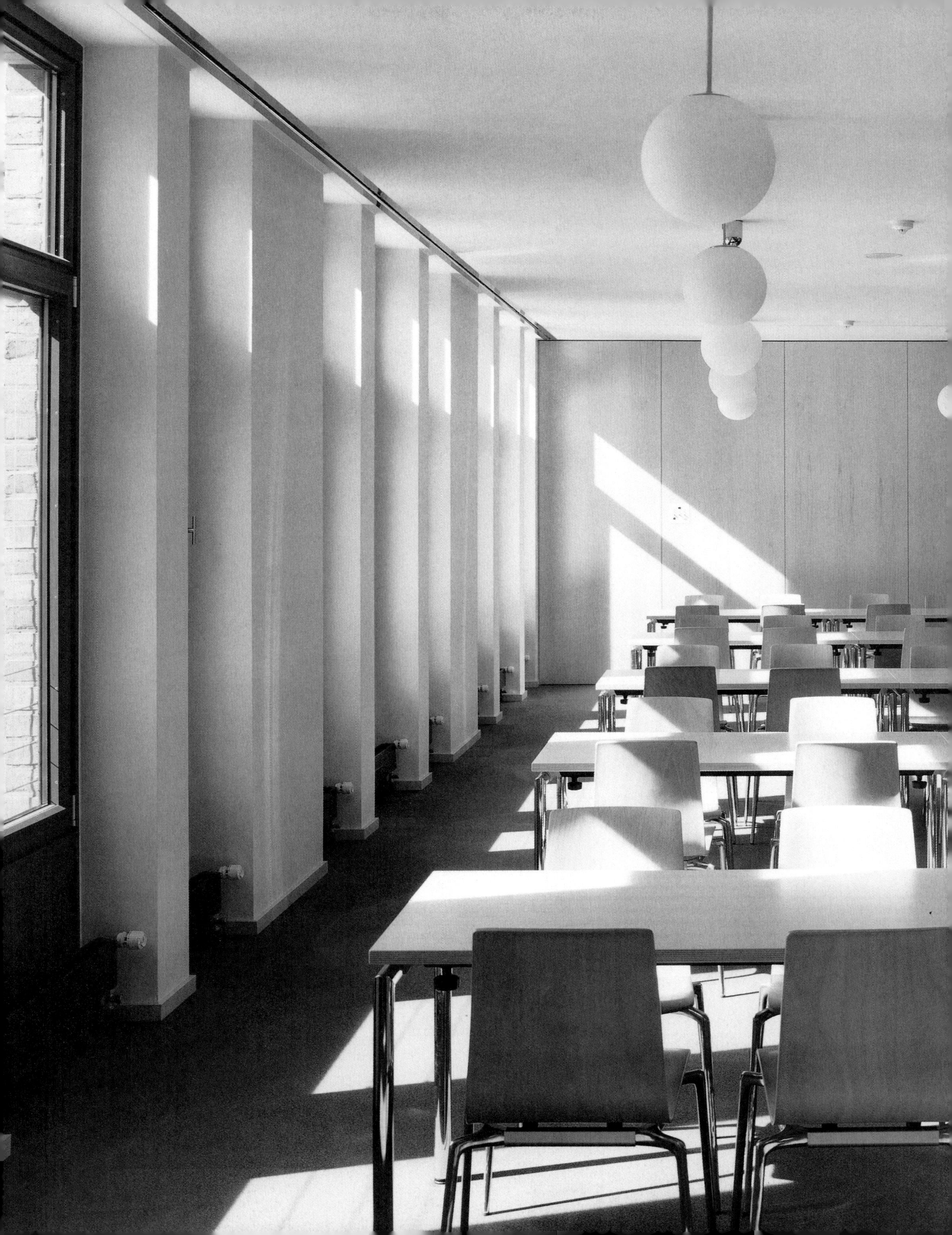

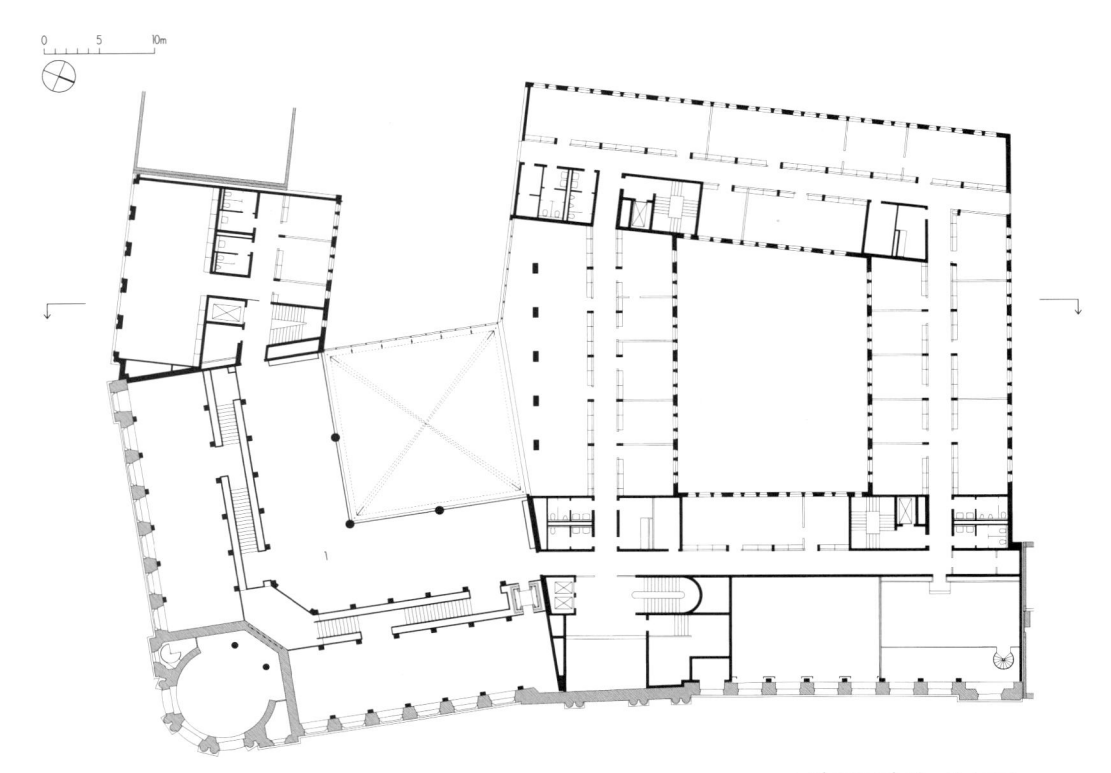

1. Obergeschoß – M 1:750

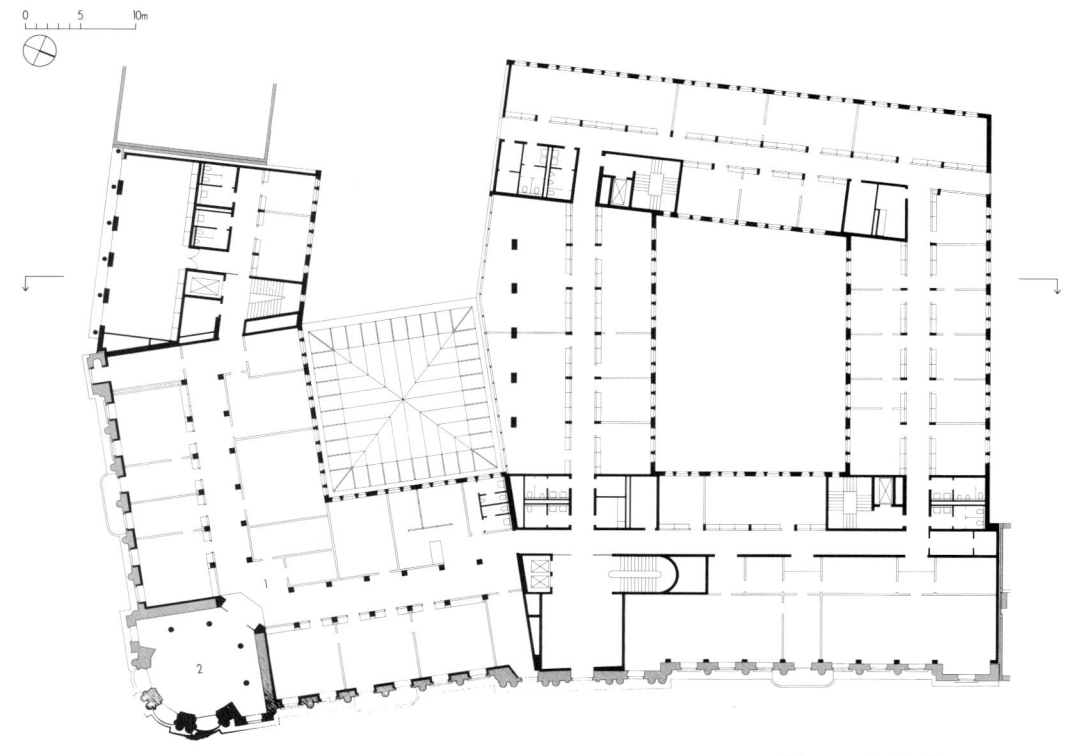

2. Obergeschoß – M 1:750

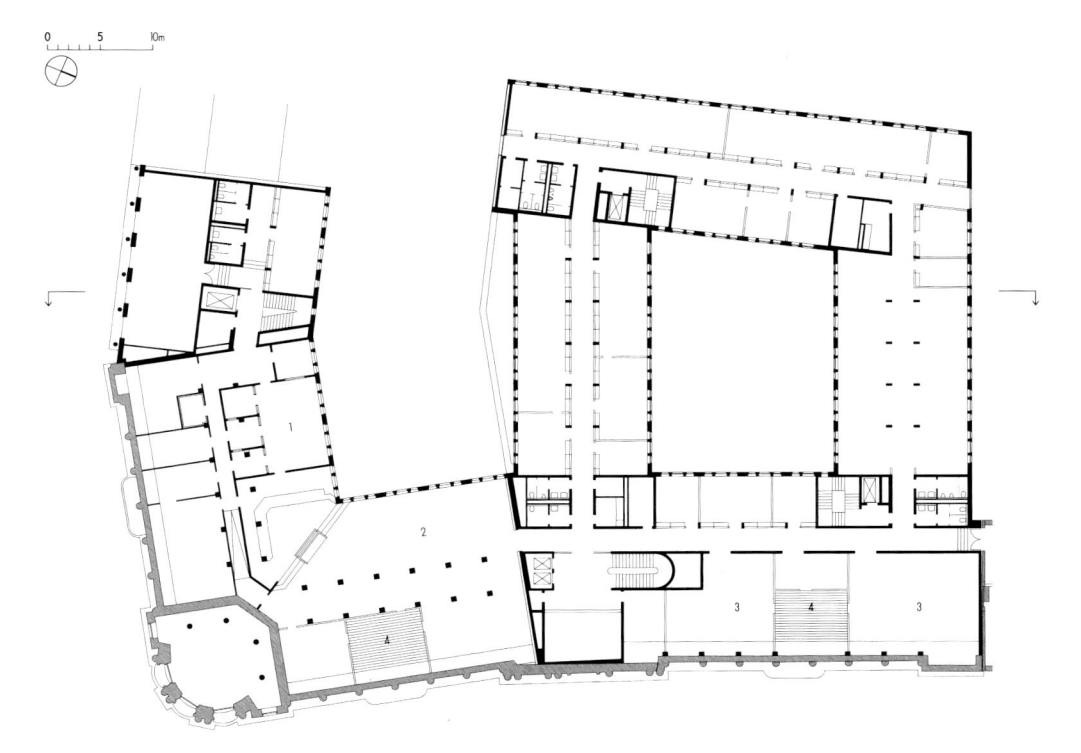

3. Obergeschoß – M 1:750

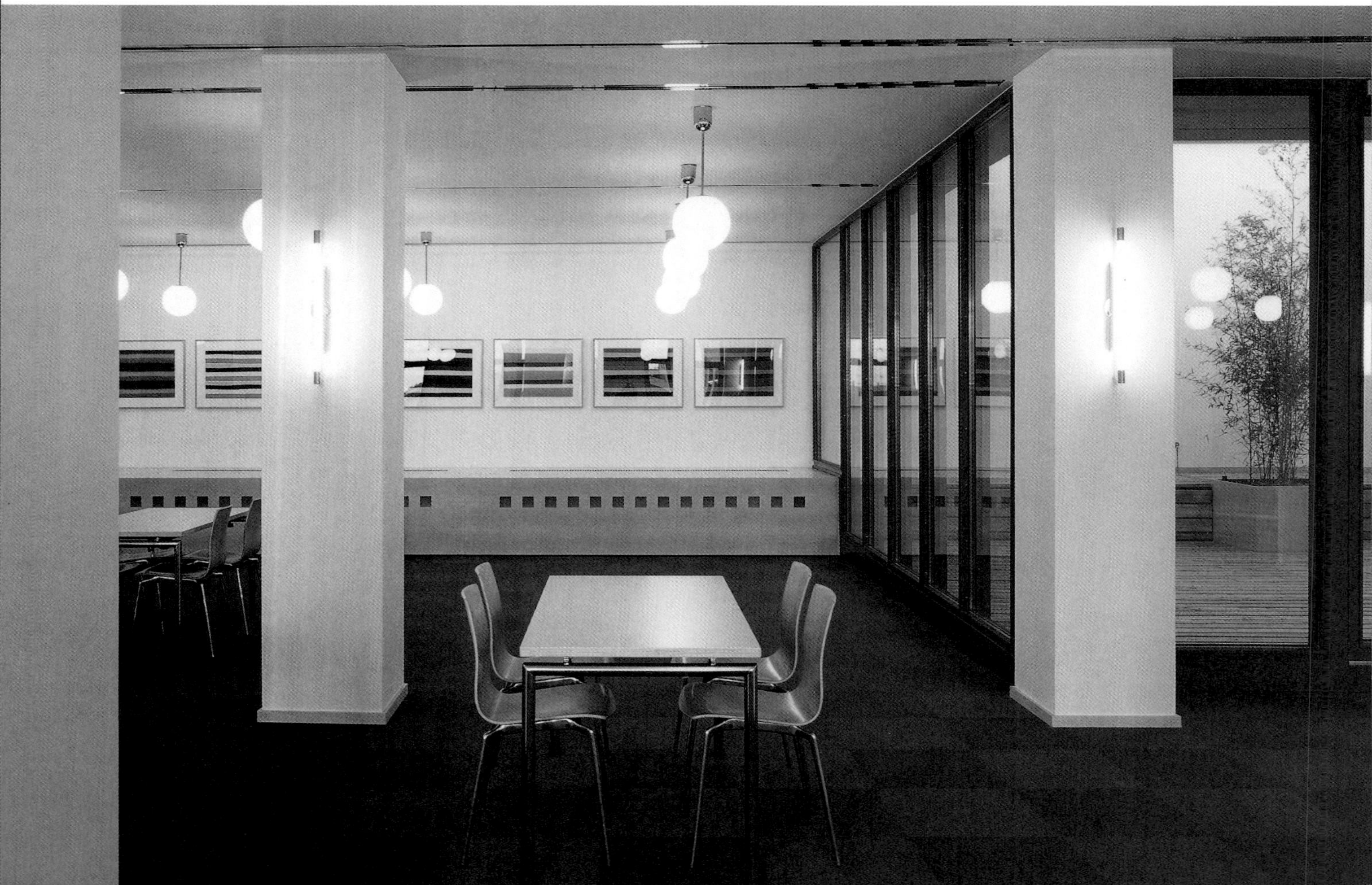

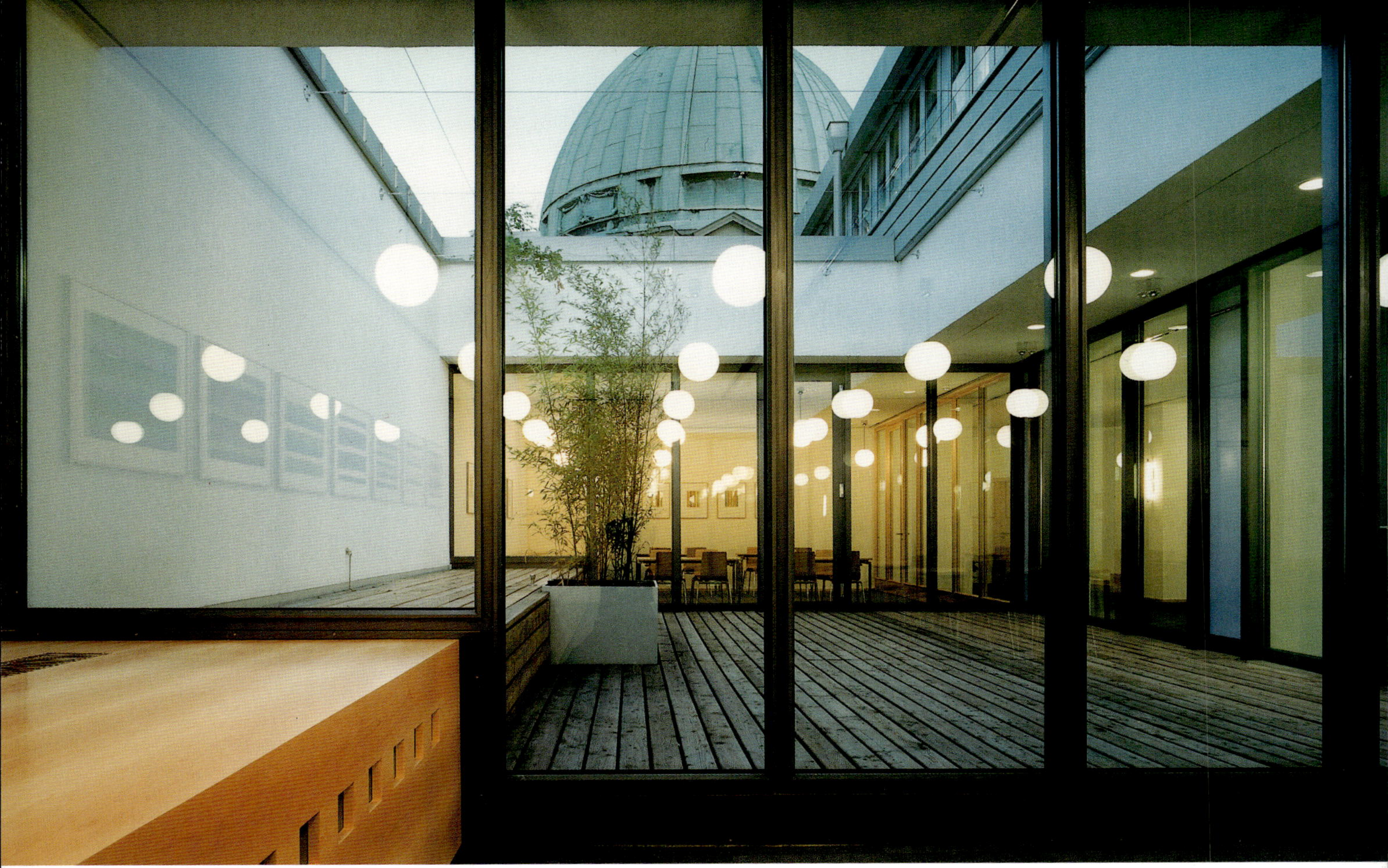

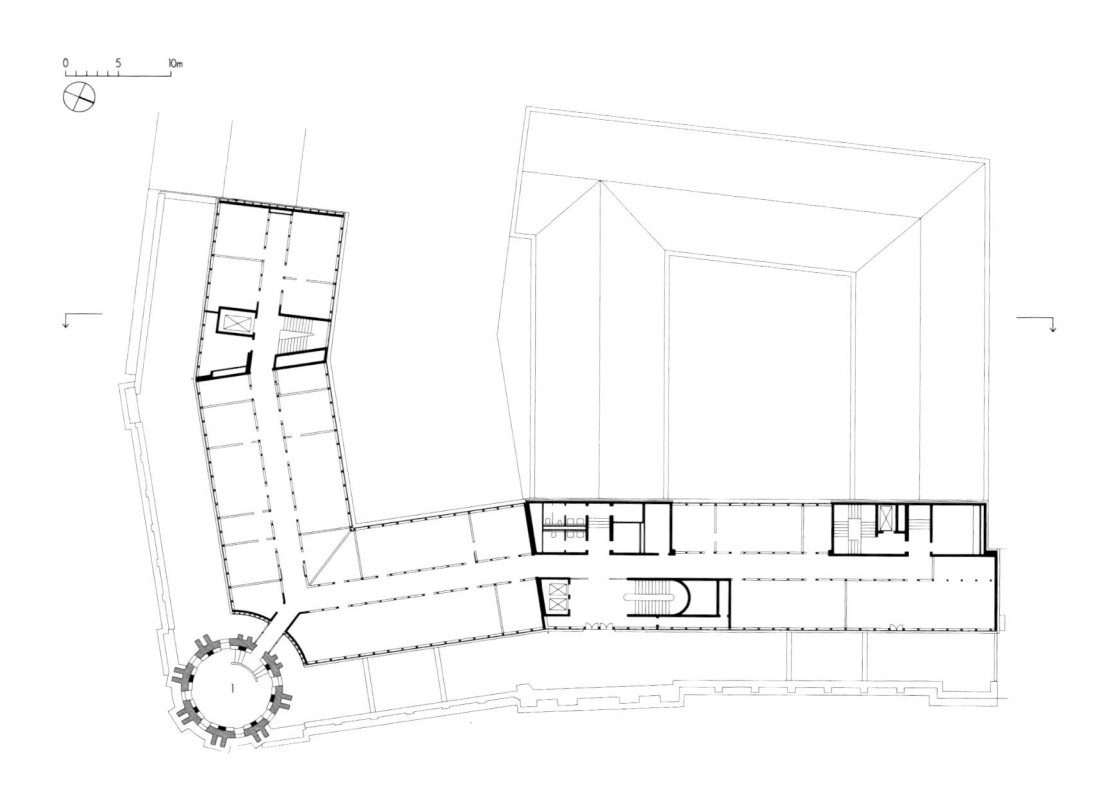

Staffelgeschoß – M 1:750

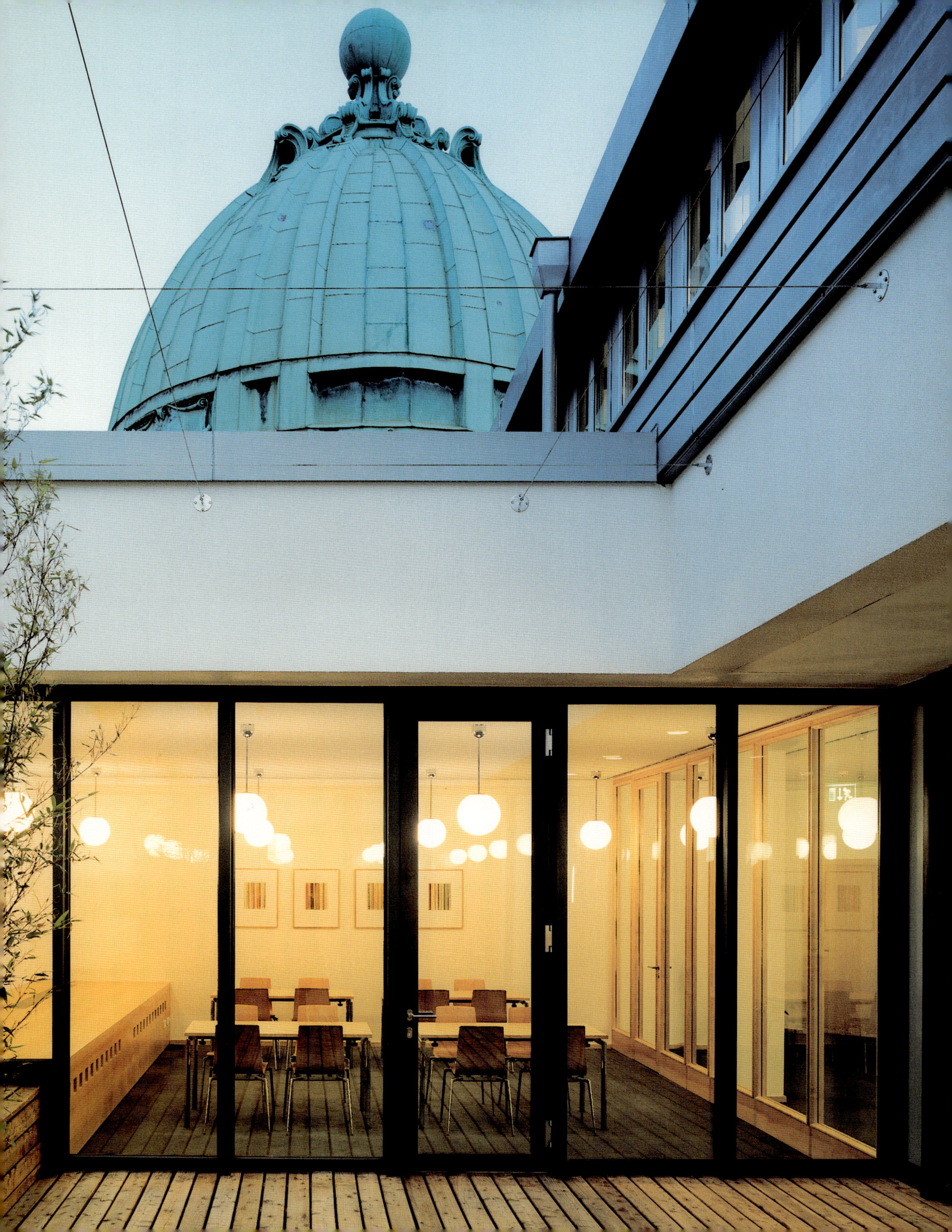

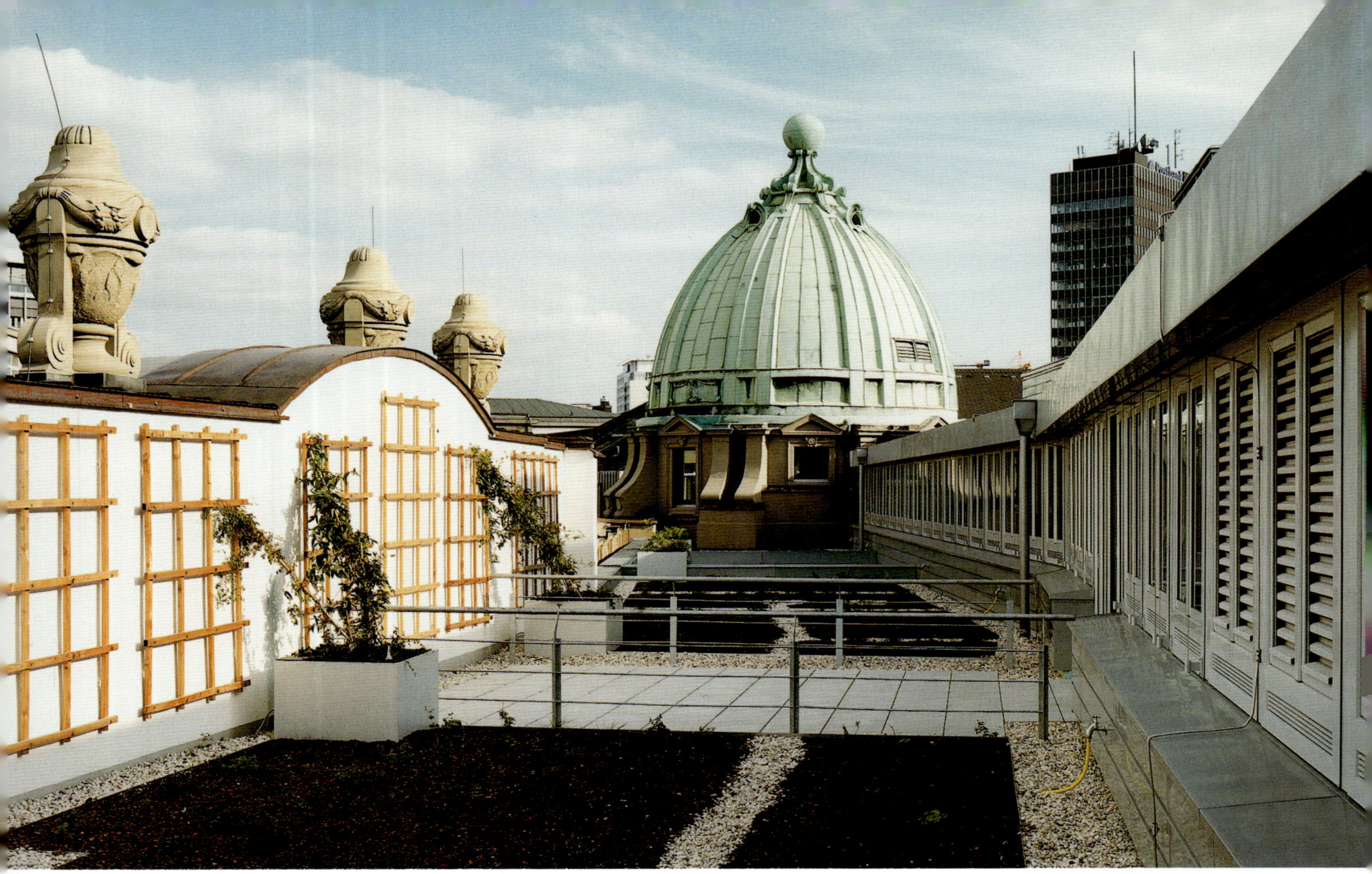

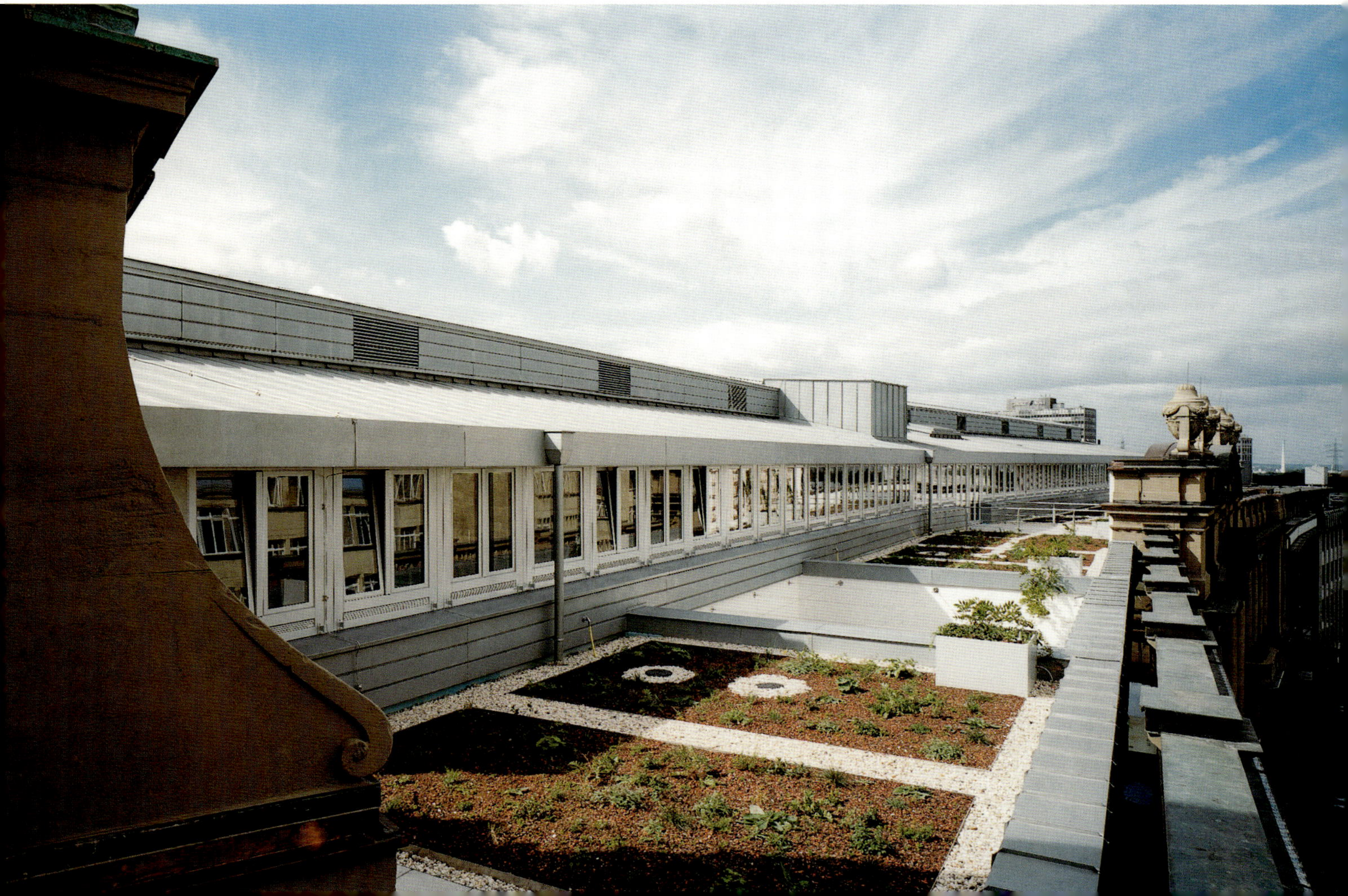

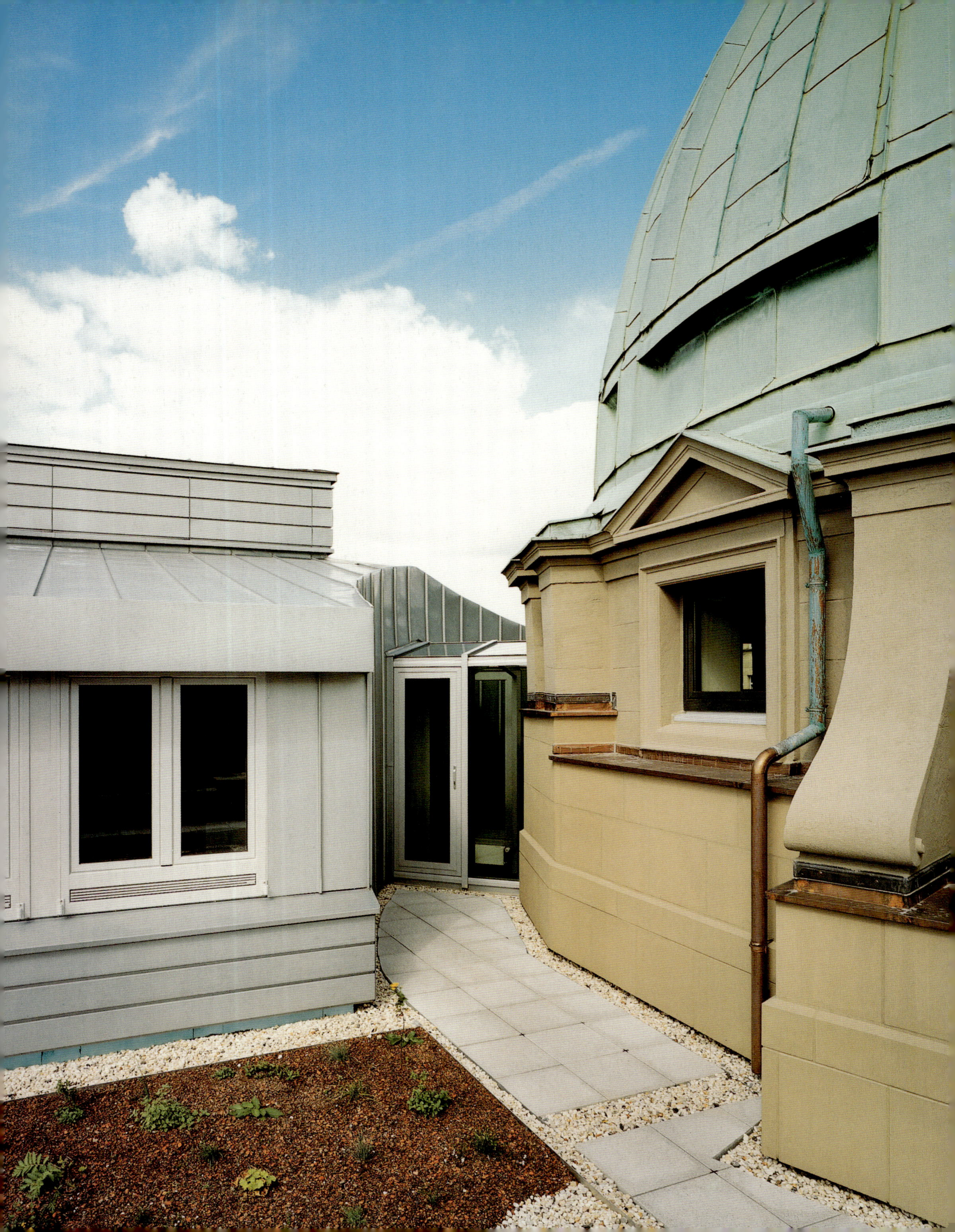

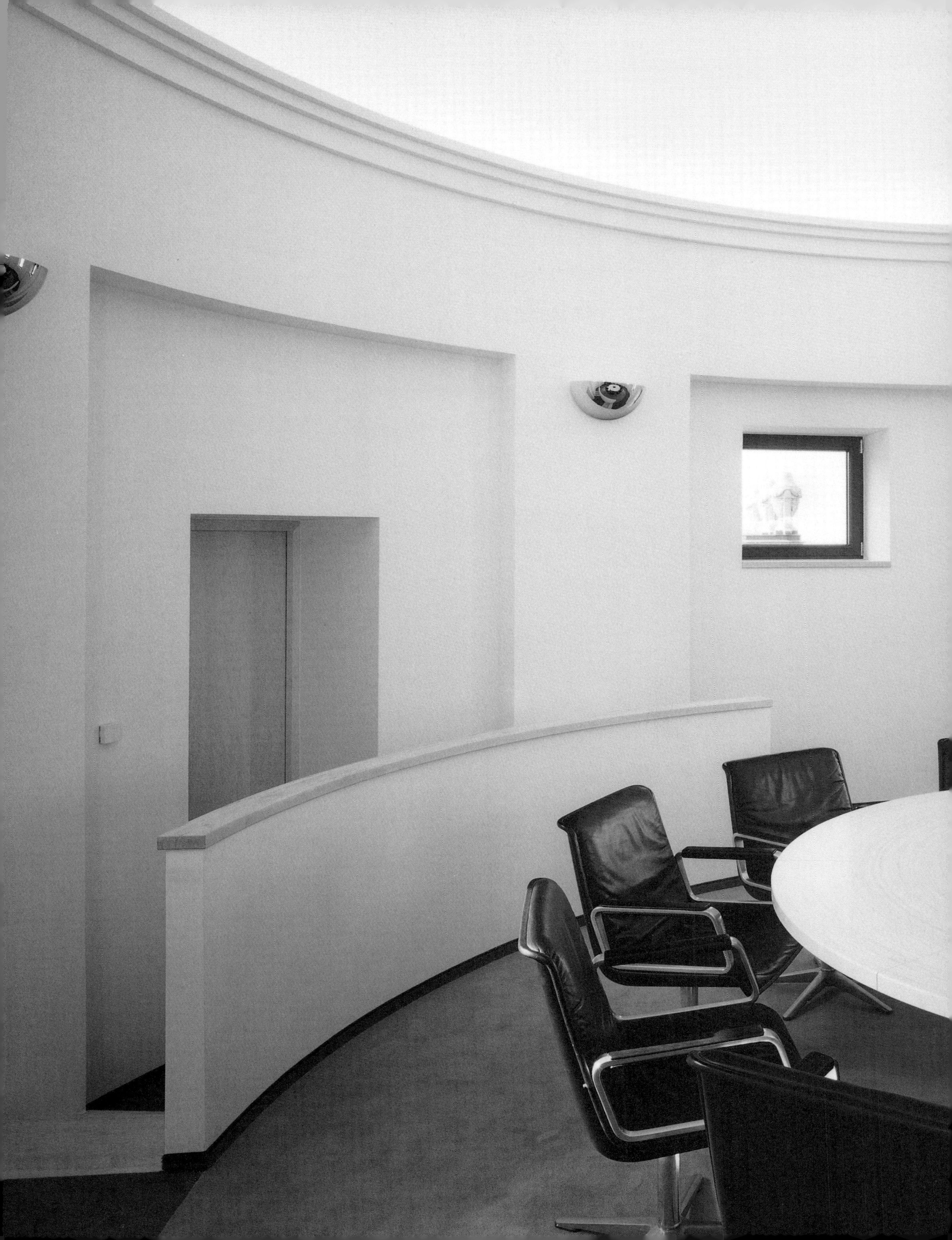

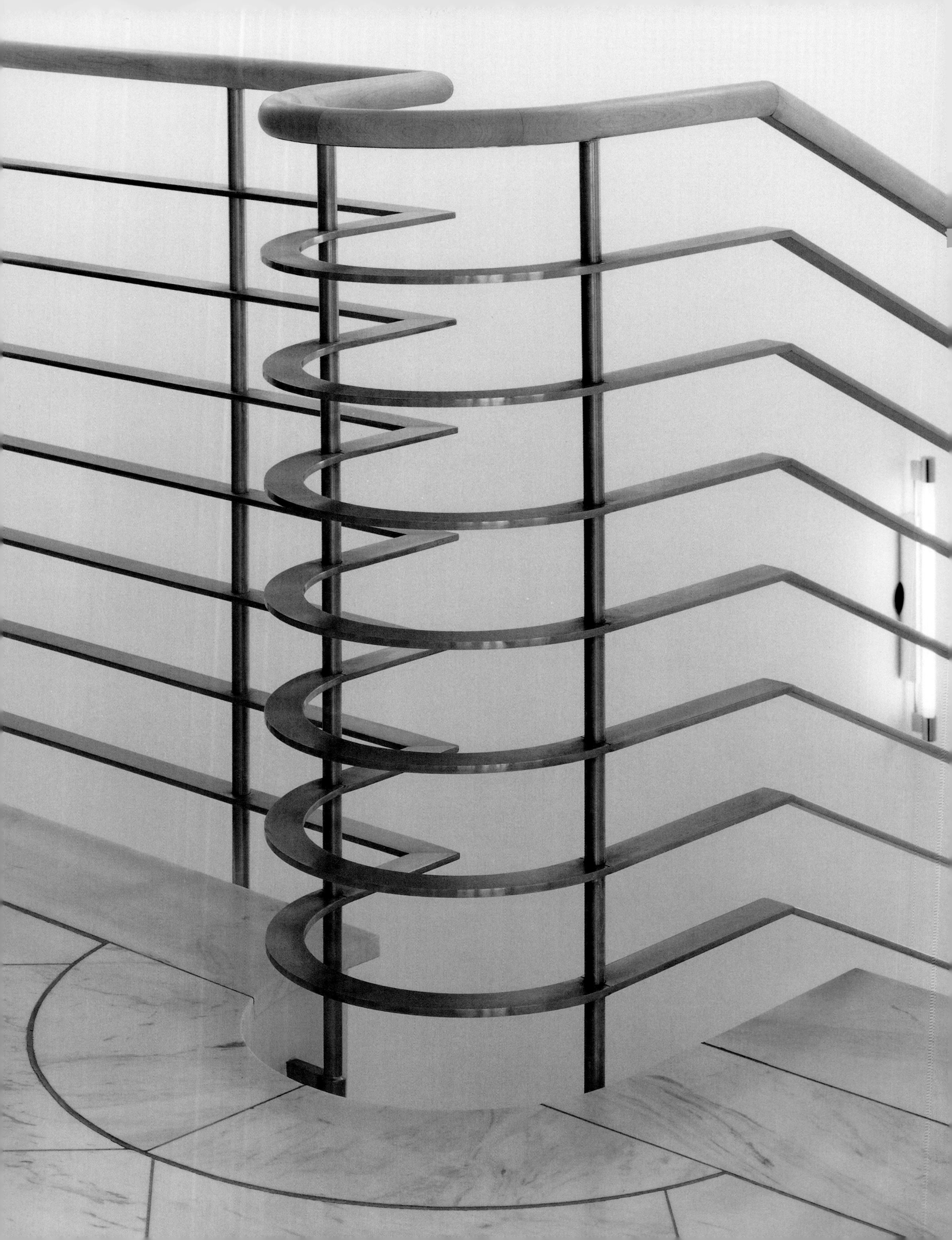

A bank is a bank is a bank ...
by Ingeborg Flagge

... would be indeed a prosaic variation for financial institutions, based on the famous line by the American poet Gertrude Stein: "A rose is a rose is a rose". In the broadest sense of a definition, a bank is an institution which deals with money: and its justified intention is to make a profit from trading with money. That, after all, is its raison d'être. At the same time, however, a bank also represents a constructed locale: a building where precisely this dealing takes place. Influential developments in the computer world have done little to alter these basic circumstances.

But changes have indeed taken place. Whereas bank functions earlier focused primarily on doing business, this has for some good time no longer been so extensively the case. For years now, banks have evolved beyond the point of being exclusively pure commercial enterprises. They have also become, to take a salient example, important patrons and collectors of the fine arts. The Deutsche Bank is a prime example of this process. Banks, indeed, have seriously cultivated their image as sponsors of the arts - in a great number and variety of areas.

These developments also provide one of the reasons why the Deutsche Bank has placed a great deal of importance on the artistry of the buildings themselves in which it does business. These approaches have become equally apparent in the restoration and revitalisation of historical buildings, and in new, contemporary building. And the times are long past in which banks sought self-glorification in the architecture which they had created for themselves - architecture which fundamentally appealed to them alone - and cared little about public opinion. In this sense, banks have truly and positively learned from the protests of the sixties and seventies.

As has always been the case, bank buildings of course essentially involve a matter of image. Today, however, banks are more likely to execute forms of constructed self-representation in collaboration with the rest of society - and not in conflict with it. And for many years, bank buildings have ceased to be temples of money: as they so obviously were in early, conservative architecture, with all their antique trappings.

One may indeed find often today that banks have commendably accepted their responsibilities for active heritage conservation, in the restoration and the further development of prominent old buildings - and have demonstrated their resolution to achieve innovative design. A noteworthy example here is the restoration and completion of the Deutsche Bank in Essen, Germany.

The most admirable approach toward heritage conservation in such cases entails learning and speaking the language of an old building, and transforming it carefully and sensitively into a contemporary building. It is precisely this art - building art - which Wilhelm Kücker has created in Essen.

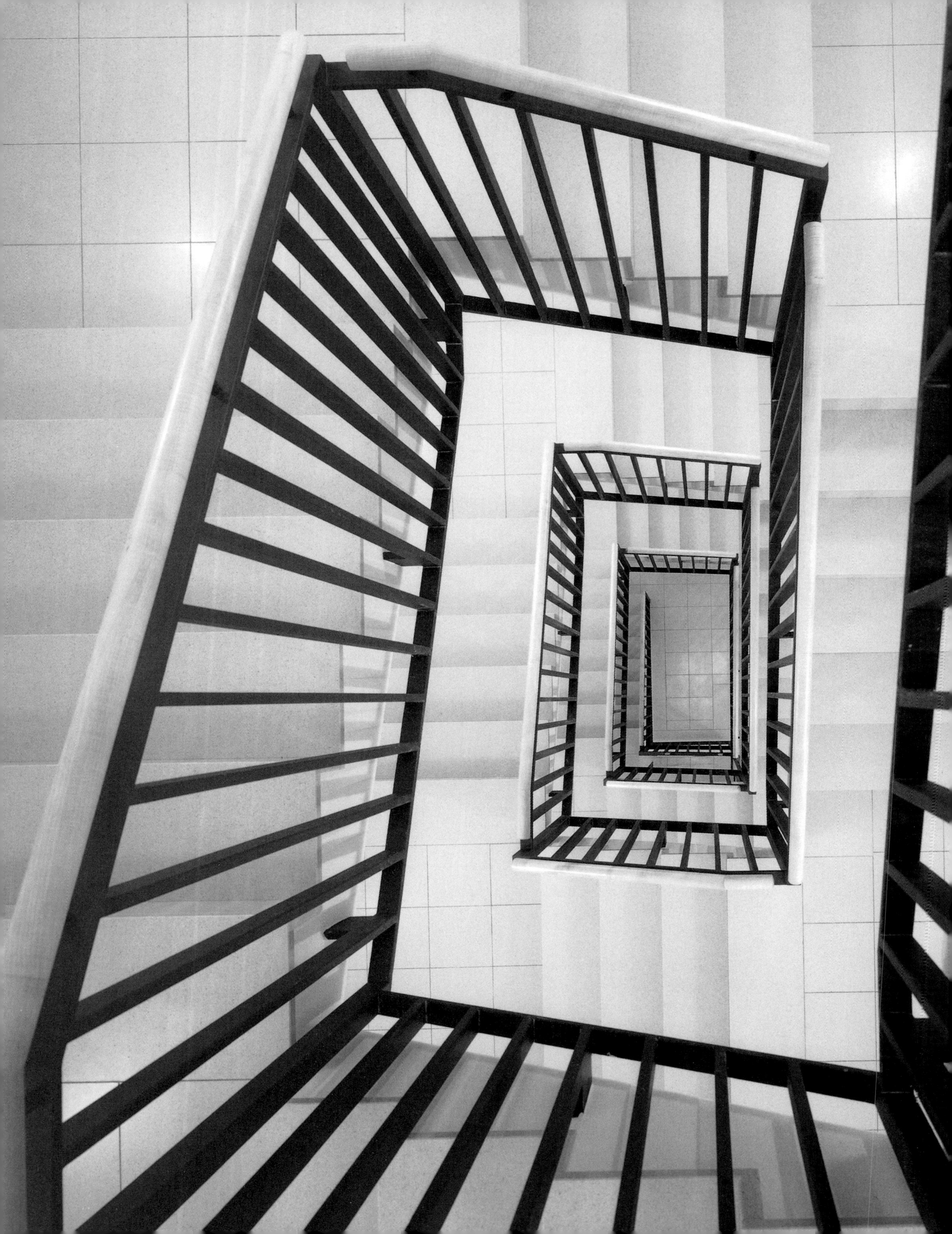

When banks build
by Ingeborg Flagge

It has been only a relatively recent phenomenon – i.e., quite late in architectural history – that institutions involved in the business of money have settled on a characteristic type of building to house their activities. In comparison to buildings intended for housing and for religious use, the history of bank buildings is actually quite young.

In ancient Egypt, it was customary to conduct payment transactions without cash: merchants and property owners, for example, maintained accounts with credits and debits at state storehouses. In classical Greece, priests were among the earliest to carry out functions resembling modern-day bankers. They deposited the valuables of others for safekeeping in temples, and granted loans in return for material remuneration. Once coins became a widespread medium of exchange, a new profession developed in Greece: that of the Trapezites. This name is derived from "trapeza" (table) in Greek: the surface on which the new class of money merchants examined, counted, and exchanged their coins. The Romans were early to recognise the profession of "argentarii" or "mensarii", as belonging to a kind of private bankers' guild. Alongside the money dealers from the state and among the priests, they carried out their lucrative business.

But these professions had not yet developed or constructed buildings designed especially for the business of dealing with money. Money, gold, and valuables belonging to the state were deposited in securely guarded vaults and treasuries. Private individuals who accumulated some form of wealth safeguarded their valuables in such repositories as chests, or they hid them in their homes. Dealing and exchange with money almost always took place in the open air: the history of bank construction therefore extends from the open marketplace table to the skyscraper of our modern day.

One of the most significant origins of our modern banks, in the form of an institution in an especially constructed building, was the trade and fair sites of Medieval Italy. Lombardic dealers were evidently among the first who set up their tables ("banca") in the marketplaces of Europe, where they checked, weighed, and exchanged coins and precious metals. Even today, "Lombard" in English usage can mean a banker or moneylender. The appellation "bancheri", or bankers, originated in the twelfth century. And, not much later, the Italian Medici, the Fuggers, the Welsers (two German families of bankers and merchants of the 14th to 17th centuries), as well as the other most influential tradesmen and private bankers, no longer conducted their professional business outside in the rain, wind and heat.

The developers of the first buildings actually constructed especially for the banking trade – for example, the Casa di San Giorgio in Genoa – had not so much convenience or prestige in mind with their grand structures: they concentrated on new activities in banking. Moneychanging gave way as prime activity to the new functions of depositing valuables, conducting bill business, and making giro transactions. The technical prerequisites for these activities were development of the bill and the banknote. A successful banker, of course, was not able to manage all these documents on small tables, or keep them in bags or money belts. He needed a solid and permanent building to store and to protect such paper instruments. Structures consequently built to provide safe deposit of such documents thus eventually became the places of commerce and exchange which we today know as banks.

The fifteenth, sixteenth, and seventeenth centuries accordingly witnessed the construction of many public, semi-public, and private buildings dedicated to the rapidly expanding business of dealing with money. Probably the oldest bill, deposit, and giro bank was the institution which opened in Barcelona in 1401. A similar bank opened in 1609 in Amsterdam, followed by the Hamburger Bank in Germany in 1619. And we may call the Bank of England, founded in 1694, the first modern commercial bank.

"Money makes the world go round" is an expression familiar to us all. But the history of money and mankind's experience with it is fleeting and uncertain. Money as a commodity is indeed ephemeral: wars and financial crashes have taught its holders that the coveted possession of money is and always has been a highly risky matter.

It is therefore no wonder that the first real bank buildings were solid and mighty structures, the design of which was intended on the purely superficial level to convey the impressions of soundness, respectability and trust. It is, moreover, more than a coincidence that the designers of these early banks patterned their creations on those building types in which business with money had flourished throughout the previous centuries: temples, cloisters, and palaces. And in the contemporary languages of many countries, evidence of such associations is still alive in such expressions as "palaces of money" or, derogatorily, "temples of mammon" (our word "mammon" derives from the Aramaic expression for possessions and riches, and is used particularly negatively in the Talmud to denote money and wealth).

"Trust is the basis for all our work" is a familiar slogan of the Deutsche Bank in Germany. This motto summarises all the impressions which bankers and the designers of banks, until the modern day, have intended bank buildings to outwardly convey: soundness and success. As a result, banks represent a mighty fortress, a reliable institution, a monumental example of solidity.

Designers of banks in the classicistic style oriented their buildings to the antique models of the Greek temple and the Roman Pantheon. The bourse in St. Petersburg, built in 1801, stands on a high footing which elevates it from the level of the profane. With the four-sided periphery of its ponderous columns and its broadly based gable, it resembles the Parthenon on the Acropolis at Athens. In 1808 John Soane patterned his building for the Bank of England, with the dome-crowned space of its great central hall, on the magnificent rotunda of the Pantheon in Rome. In both, the vast domes vividly call to mind the vault of the heavens.

Entry into these consecrated halls of monetary exchange is a solemnly celebrated process. Those entering here leave behind the irreverent world of the street, climb high steps, and pass through broad portals into another world.

Inside as well, these edifices resemble monumental shrines and sanctuaries. Coffered ceilings, massive marble, and decorative plasterwork recall the characteristics which authorities beginning with Vitruvius prescribed as the essence of superior architecture. These early authors, of course, had no vision of the prime characteristics of bank buildings as we have come to know them: stability, utility, and beauty. It is in this form language that the self-expression of banks finds common ground with the expectations of their clientele with respect to security and representation.

Once classicism gave way to historicism in architecture, mixture and imitation of all styles of building history began on an extensive scale. As was the case for all prestigious buildings of the nineteenth century, architects for banks also resorted to those models from architectural history which were best capable of evincing feelings of harmony and invincibility: and examples were taken above all from the Renaissance and Baroque periods. It is, moreover, especially the mundane ponderousness and fortified permanence of these buildings, with their weighty rusticated ashlar, which radiate dignity and solemnity and which thereby reflect the self-esteem of the institutions which they enclose. The Gothic style, on the other hand – with its more delicate and filigree-like impressions – has rarely served as a model for bank buildings.

In any case, to be sure, architecture always reflects the time in which it originates and develops. With the advent of new materials such as concrete and cast iron in the nineteenth century, opportunities for new construction became available – and the design of bank buildings underwent a logical change. Banks became cathedrals of innovative architecture. On the outside, the impression of pompous solemnity continued to dominate. On the interior, however, the mass and the dignity of classic architecture with its allegoric reliefs and antique statues yielded to the lightness of the great train-station concourses of the era. Great glass domes span huge, high cashiers' lobbies which, with their bright spaciousness – and together with their open ambulatories often stretching over several building storeys, their cast-iron latticework, their counters sophisticated in their very simplicity, and their coloured-glass windows – create the impression of transparent cathedrals. The Bank Credit Lyonnais in Paris is possibly one of the loveliest spaces constructed around the last turn of the century. With the great span of its celebrated interior, symmetrically configured around the entrance to the great safe, it calls to mind gigantic greenhouses and railway-station concourses.

Similar grandiose roles are shared in these cathedrals of commerce by the wide staircases, the great clocks, and the distinct and eloquent built-in units. These overpowering rooms virtually celebrate their own huge spans and the new materials which had become available to build them. In contrast, the Vienna Postal Savings Bank (Postsparkassenamt) which Otto Wagner built in 1906 represents the functional alternative. On the outside, the bank appears as a large building mass which presents tranquil lines. On the inside, the white tellers' lobby with its simplicity and its clarity of organisation makes an almost abstract impression. This room pays no obeisance whatsoever to history or to the outward physical representation of banks which had been previously known and favoured. Otto Wagner's Postal Savings Bank is remarkably characterised by reduction in colours and forms, elegance by virtue of the absence of flourish in the tellers' lobby, and lack of embellishment in the great glass ceiling. As such, Wagner's bank epitomises a new and modern form of representation – one which, however, found only very few adherents in the following years.

The 1920s – halcyon days for the avant-garde and for modernism in architecture – were years of economic turbulence and depression. Galloping inflation and stock-market crashes distracted bankers from any ideas which they might otherwise have had about innovative new buildings. During this period, there was accordingly hardly any construction of modern bank buildings worthy of note or mention.

After the Second World War, it was above all the new bank buildings whose quiet and simple forms spoke the language of modernism. The constructed gestures of power evident in the old banking houses had become a thing of the past. Banks opted for functional representation and against awe-inspiring expressions of dignity and distinction. During the course of massive post-war construction, however, the prevalent style of simple building rapidly degenerated to a state of unimaginative impoverishment. Indeed: in the context of faceless grid architecture of the sixties and seventies, banks were no longer distinguishable from any other of the unrefined and functionalistic buildings of the time. During this period, standardisation in building caught up with the banks as well.

In the student revolts which took place during the 1970s, one of the prime targets for rage in demonstrations was the destruction of the city by roadway construction in favour of automobile convenience. Another of these targets was banks. There were basically two phenomenon which gave rise in this context to the voicing of harsh criticism and the development of mistrust. One was the predominance of glass façades in architecture: although they provide an outward appearance of openness, they nevertheless seal the interior of buildings off from the city and its population, and thereby remain at a good distance from them. The other phenomenon is the tendency of banks to reach to the heavens, in taller and taller buildings – and to seek a new symbolic identity in ever higher skyscrapers. Bank skyscrapers of the seventies and eighties are, for the most part, banal and conspicuous solitaires in the urban architectural landscape, just as faceless as they are inordinate. The individual member of society – i.e., the patron of the banks – felt more repelled than solicited, more disquieted than appealed to as a fellow citizen. A great number of these buildings spoke the language of arrogance, not of trustworthiness. An early exception from this rule, to be sure, was the internationally famous Hong Kong and Shanghai Bank built by Norman Foster. By virtue of its highly individual and impressive design, it became the trademark of Hong Kong during the 1980s.

As have the participants in our economy in general, banks over the past few years have rediscovered the message which architecture represents. In the context of the discussion on corporate identity, banks are seriously considering their own constructed form and the effects conveyed by this form. The modern bank is a pure service provider: in its role as employer it is just as important toward the corporate inside as it is in its outward effects on the city. In days of yore, consultation with clients of the bank provided the focal point of bank business. Today, self-service in the bank is just as essential as in the supermarket. Oral communication at the bank counter and the teller's window has been replaced by new media. The site of confidential discussion of money matters has shifted to a technology centre.

The consequences of these developments for the architecture of banks is just as variegated and non-uniform as is the entire spectrum of post-modern construction. The range is indeed great: from the vibrant organic forms of the Nederlandsche Middenstandsbank in Amsterdam (by Alberts and van Huut, 1987) to the eccentric national bank in Fribourg, Switzerland (by Mario Botta,

1982); and from the meaningful, gigantic urban villa of the Regional Central Bank in Potsdam, Germany (by Ortner + Ortner, 1996), to the naked, rationalistic cube of the Regional Central Bank in Leipzig (by Hans Kollhoff, 1996).

Many of these new bank buildings have been built in suburbs or on the periphery of urban centres: downtown areas nowadays rarely offer enough space for new building. When banks do find a niche in midtown neighbourhoods, it is not seldom in old buildings which they restore and remodel in accordance with heritage requirements, and which they extend by annexes in harmony with their traditional history and development. In such manner, they make a locally appropriate contribution to preservation of the urban landscape. Just such a contribution has been made by the Deutsche Bank in Essen.

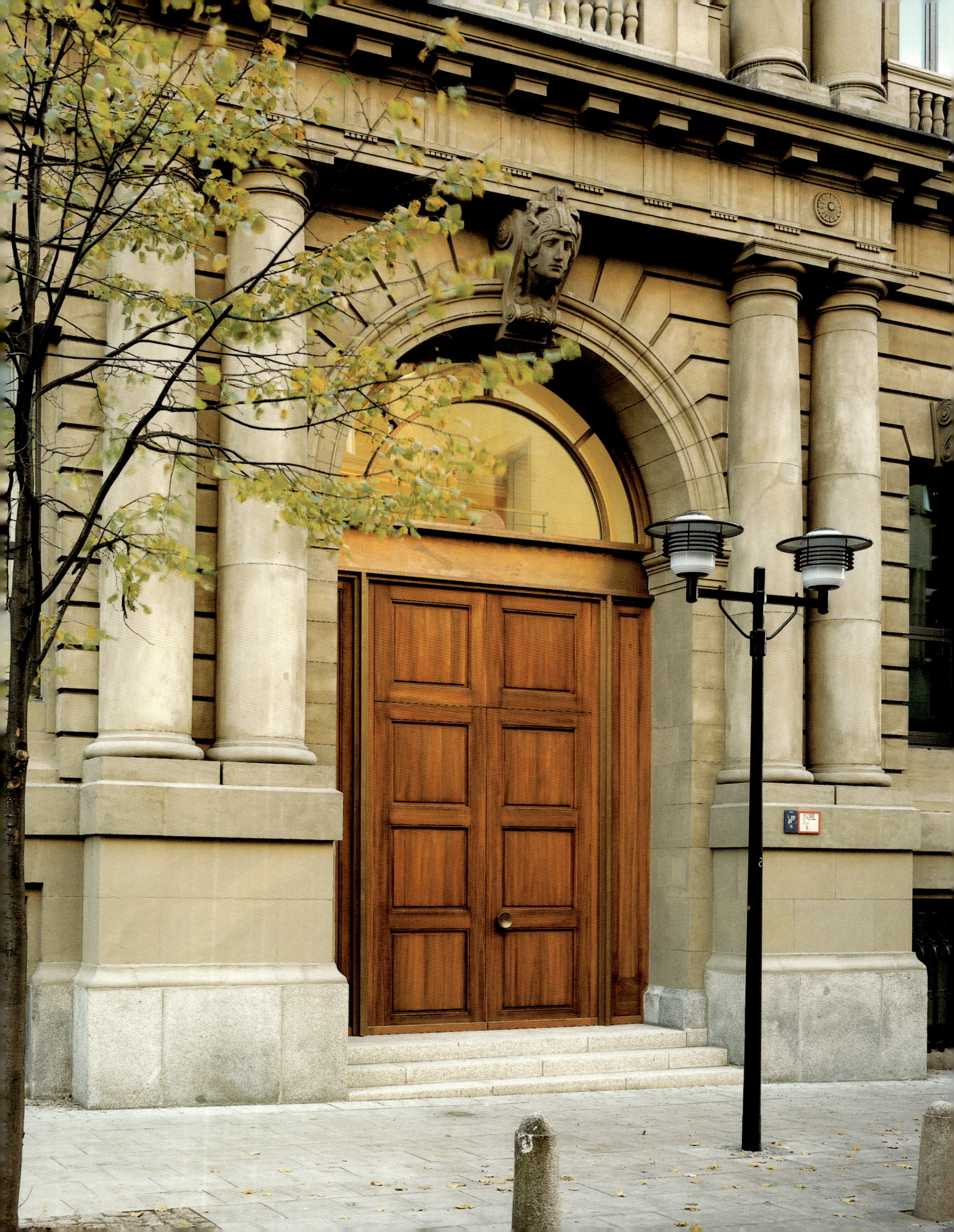

Renovation and New Construction by the Architect Wilhelm Kücker: the Deutsche Bank Building in Essen, Germany, 1993–1997
by Wilfried Wang

Extensively today, one may justifiably interpret the prime mission of contemporary architecture in the compacted urban context to represent an increasingly significant constituent in the processes of conservation, of stratification, of partial renewal and – in some cases – of demolition. To the extent to which this aspect is valid, projects such as that for renovation and new construction of the Deutsche Bank complex in Essen may be considered as veritable indicators for the sensitiveness of content and design with which developers and architects approach such challenges. The realisation that today it is not necessary – or even feasible – to build everything anew, from the ground up, determines to a growing extent the attitude of those responsible for construction efforts: i.e., it reveals precisely the responsiveness with which these participants perceive the form and substance of their work.

We all know how insensitively existing building substance was treated in Germany during the 1960s and 1970s. High rooms built around the turn off the century were adapted by installation of suspended ceilings to prevailing fashions in horizontal spatial configurations. Decorative plasterwork – or, at least, what remained of it after the Second World War – was sacrificed to dominating ideals of purity, as expressed in classic modernism. The simple spatial effects earlier preferred, as well as clearly structured room sequences, gave way to intentionally anti-axial thoroughfare layouts.

During renovation carried out between 1971 and 1975, a number of just such modifications was inflicted on the building on the corner of Maxstrasse and Lindenallee in Essen, which Peter Zindel had built in 1901 for the Essener Creditanstalt, a bank corporation founded in 1872. Wilhelm Mertens, in the meantime, had extended the bank along Lindenstrasse in 1908. Mertens, who was also the architect for the home office of the Deutsche Bank in Berlin, succeeded in expanding Zindel's original building, originally based on a diagonal axis, by adding a middle section projecting from the front of the building, as new unit to the complex: a supplement in harmony with the architectural language originally expressed by the corner rotunda. Mertens' expansion in 1908 very shortly afterward – hardly seven years had passed since the rotunda addition – was successful to such an extent that reservations so prevalent in our day against such an approach – i.e., in the form of extremely critical attitudes against direct assumption of architectural language for building additions – are hardly in order. Today, as then, the prime objective of the architects and developers for this bank building has been to preserve the unity of this noteworthy building.

Just as Mertens had attempted to achieve unity in the façades of this building, a prime determining factor for Zindel and Mertens was the spatial penetration of the building substance, through to the façade. The fact that the magnificence of Zindel's palatial architecture – with the sumptuous offices of the Board of Directors, and with their six metre high ceilings – extended consistently on the level of the ground floor, from the street all the way through to the courtyard side, was in all likelihood a major design problem even for Mertens in his day. Indeed: he implemented stairways on the rear side of the building to reduce the height of the ceilings in the prestigious storeys from their original five and six and a half metres, to something more than three metres. Mertens consequently doubled the number of floors originally designed by Zindel for use on the street side of the building.

The Deutsche Bank acquired this building in 1925. As a result of the damage from the Second World War and extensive renovations during the early 1970s, nothing remained of the original sophisticated spatial structure realised by Zindel and Mertens. By the early 1990s, the users of this building had become sufficiently aware of the problematic nature of the hodgepodge of variously designed building sections, each with their own ceiling heights and the associated differences in levels. It was consequently decided to carry out basic restructuring of the entire building – which in any case again required new restoration measures owing to its age. Exact cost comparisons conducted for the alternatives of extensive restoration and of new construction supported the decision to extensively reconstruct the bank facilities on the corner – while maintaining the still-extant façades created by Zindel and Mertens, officially protected as they are as architectural heritage. This study estimated the costs for extensive restoration – i.e., for maintaining the existing main usable floor area of 6,671 square meters – at 47.6 million Deutsche marks. For extensive reconstruction, resulting in new main usable floor area of 8,600 square meters, the study estimated costs at 76 million Deutsche marks. This latter, preferred alternative, although more expensive, would have yielded a gain in usable floor space of slightly less than 30%.

During the course of the considerations made for new structuring of the building, the architect and developer examined a great number of approaches toward finding optimal solutions. In the early 1990s, the building owners conducted a limited competition and had expert studies conducted on the building. These efforts enabled a gradual process leading toward a definition of use of the future building. These studies also disclosed the two primary challenges directed to the architects invited to participate in the competition: the polygonal form of the property subdivision, as well as the requirements posed by the existing façades. Despite the evidently difficult search for a solution optimal from all aspects, the parties bearing responsibility for the building developer arrived at a decision in favour of the proposal submitted by Wilhelm Kücker. The Architectural Advisory Board – consisting of Thomas Herzog, Vittorio Magnago Lampugnani and the author of the present article – arrived at conclusions in support of a decision for Kücker. After a planning and execution period of four years, the reconstruction project was turned over on schedule to the building users.

With respect to its fundamental arrangement, Wilhelm Kücker's design is planned in accordance with a self-evident solution: one which, in retrospect, is perplexing in its simplicity. Simple and self-evident as it may seem to Kücker and us, however, this solution evidently managed to evade all of those who had made previous such attempts.

Kücker's first dominant decision pertained to the idealisation of courtyard structures: representing not only the diagonally symmetric reconstruction of the corner volume of the former Zindel building, but also the very first achievement of logical consummation of the Mertens Block. In his solution, Kücker by no means evaded any of the difficulties posed by the angularities of the building property. He did not allow these angularities, to be sure, to impair the interior sequence of rooms or the clarity of the appearance made by the building structure in its entirety. The building extension on Maxstrasse has accordingly been adapted to the constraints posed by this street, as has the west wing in accordance with the property boundary. As a result, the possible future extension of this wing toward Maxstrasse would allow for the consolidation of the entire building complex.

By his inclusion of a generously proportioned main banking hall, Wilhelm Kücker in his design for the Deutsche Bank building in Essen has succeeded in breaking up the urban-design and architectural tension created by the constraints of the existing corner rotunda. This lobby indeed represents a room whose content and space fulfil the expectations made by the imposing building dome: unique as it is in the present skyline of Essen. It may well be that such expectations held by many of the people of Essen who use this building are exaggerated – and that they do in fact represent somewhat of an anachronism in today's world. Banks today, after all, hardly need such a lobby, since the automated teller machines in Germany are usually located outside in their own special anterooms, just inside the main bank entrance. But it is precisely differences such as these among institutions which commit certain of them to the conservation of traditions – and which symbolise cultural distinctions which some clients consciously or unconsciously prefer. Other patrons, on the contrary, are prompted by such distinctions to favour forms of rationalistic consistency characterised by cool or even somtimes unfriendly abstraction.

Certainly, this banking hall – with its steel portals calling to mind the steel mills of the region – is a luxury from the standpoint of the building developers. But in its overall relationship to the enclosed space of the bank complex, its benefits are greater than its costs. From this standpoint as well, the banking hall has reaped severalfold what was invested in it.

In this manner, the original building components – with highly intentional consideration taken of the expectations placed on them – have played a major role in realisation of the new complex. The role played by the banking hall is indeed paradigmatic, down to the last detail, for all the relationships between old and new in the Deutsche Bank building. A walk through the rooms of the complex impressively reveals these links between the rhythmically spatial constraints of the heritage-protected façades, and the newly constructed offices and common rooms.

These old façades by no means hide what has come to be so widespread in such buildings nowadays: i. e., storeys which are arranged according to their own inherent principles, which cut through tall windows, or which are crammed to the walls full of modern technology. Instead, Wilhelm Kücker's design has implemented an astonishingly simple solution which takes full advantage of the grandiose room dimensions. By means of an equally grandiose new stairway complex, Kücker has harmonised these room proportions with the new, normal storey structure.

This unconventional double stairway complex forms a transparent spatial layer between the high rooms on the ground floor toward the street, and the two galleries facing the tellers' lobby. Thanks to set-back conference cubicles, visitors and users on this level experience the galleries as equally transparent spaces. All these elements of the bank complex go to produce a continuous spatial quality: one which could hardly be imagined by experiencing the exterior stone façades alone. The surprise produced on the interior, however, is all the more refreshing as a result. Indeed: this combination of astonishingly simple spatial solutions and open spatial quality is indeed stimulating in comparison to conventional contemporary architecture.

This renovation, revitalisation and refreshment of the original complex, however, would not have succeeded without the fitting respect shown by Wilhelm Kücker in observance of the constraints presented by the originally existing building complex. A review of the many designs presented by Kücker's predecessors – going all the way back to Zindel and Mertens – clearly reveals that the renewed building as it now stands exhibits a quality which existed at no previous time on this corner: neither as actual building state nor as conceived design. One may accordingly and justifiably conclude that the present state of the structure not only represents an absolute enhancement with respect to its preceding conditions, but that it – with its spatial quality and typology – will go down in architectural history as an example truly worthy of emulation.

In his overall solution, Wilhelm Kücker resolved a great number of potential interior-space conflicts by application of reservation and lightness. One example here is the redesign of the entrance areas in the corner rotunda and in the middle section projecting from the front of the building. Since the old entrance level lay above the basement, and since the owners understandably had the entrance level lowered to that of the street, it was necessary for the architect to completely redesign the stairway in the middle projecting section of the building. With respect to their material characteristics, the craftsmanship with which they were created and in their dimensions, both the huge new doors as well as the symmetric stairway complex reflect the attitude expressed in the original façade. The craftsmanship of the brass and oak for the doors, the naturally appropriate workmanship evident in the curved marble for the stairway parapet, and the mezzanines with their fittingly generous dimensions all endow the entrance and access area with an atmosphere of nobility. And this atmosphere is surely not exaggerated: it, after all, performs the service of satisfactorily affording a logical transition from the outside to the interior – from the metropolitan street front to the contemporary individual offices inside.

The executives at the Deutsche Bank in Essen likewise enjoy the benefits of Kücker's respect for tradition. Like the first upper storey, the piano nobile on the former second upper storey was preserved on the street side from the fate of being eliminated by floors inserted through the tall windows. After completion of rebuilding, the branch-office directors will remain on this level. Above this level, behind the roof parapet walls, Kücker arranged the common rooms and separated them by installation of atria. As a result, the staff cafeteria and training rooms enjoy natural daylight and a pleasant view outward.

The remarks made here until this point have exclusively dealt with the consequences faced by Kücker in observing the heritage constraints placed on the street-side façade. The bank itself, moreover, set extremely difficult stipulations entailing the use of their rooms. The users expected highly flexible employment of the new office space. For the eventuality that the Deutsche Bank did not require all the floor space in the complex, the developer required the architect to provide in his design for independent access to additional rooms by outside companies. Since, however, the prestigious character of the entrances from the corner of Maxstrasse and Lindenallee, and from the middle section projecting from the front of the building, did not really allow access to the building by out-of-house firms, Kücker designed an uninterrupted entrance on the courtyard side of the building – access also able to be used by the fire department and rescue squads in case of emergency. This entrance has such an open and accessible character that its use for passage to offices used by other companies would by no means give the impression of sneaking in the back door.

If one may generally consider the results of this project to represent a successful synthesis of existing building substance and exacting new stipulations, then it would perhaps be justified to consider the new façade facing Maxstrasse – as extension of Zindel's south façade – to be the outer expression of this general synthesis, as well as a veritable litmus test for Wilhelm Kücker's qualities as an architect. Here as well, Kücker has succeeded in endowing the new components of the building added by him with linking functions as well as a relatively independent quality.

In the rebuilt Deutsche Bank, horizontally configured masonry encloses the installed steel-frame construction. This construction expresses the rhythmic and spatial structure of the rebuilt building. Differentiation of the infilling within this steel frame in turn calls attention to the adjacent coarse and fine rusticated ashlar. The coarse layering of the infilling, with flush bond in the rebuilt part of the complex, accordingly corresponds to the deep rustication of the ground storey. The set-back infilling of the new third and fourth upper storeys, with the now free-standing round columns, corresponds to the column arrangement of the first upper storey of the Zindel building. The round openings in the Vierendeel beam which spans the garage and fire accessway likewise represent an echo of the round arches of the adjoining façade. This Vierendeel beam, in addition, satisfies so to speak an expectation aroused by modern architecture: liberating spatial effects and compression of historical experience.

The three round windows equally serve as a point of departure and as denouement for the entire bank complex. Like the overall design, they represent a congenial conjuncture of appropriate solution approaches: one which unites the satisfaction of functional requirements and expectations for prestigious impression.

Apprehension was truly great at the beginning of consideration for renovation of the Deutsche Bank building in Essen. Over the years since renovation first began, the many architectural designs submitted had the effect of disquieting rather than convincing those responsible for operation of the bank. Under these conditions, congratulations are all the more in order to the developers for their steadfastness in search for a solution, to the many craftsmen for their professional achievements and of course to the architect Wilhelm Kücker and his team for their exemplary solution. It is not always the case in the architectural world that whatever proves longest will prove best – but in the case of the Deutsche Bank building in Essen, we can state that this rule applies.

Deutsche Bank Essen

Bauherr
DEBEKO Immobilien GmbH
& Co Grundbesitz OHG, Eschborn
Projektleiter: Ulrich Krantz

Architekt
Wilhelm Kücker, München – Berlin
mit Klaus Freudenfeld (Projektleiter bis September 1996)
und Giuseppe Battaglia, Henning Bouterwek, Waltraut Heim,
Nicolas Hein, Norbert Schöfer, Thomas Schulz,
Christa Landmann, Frank Feuchtenbeiner
Örtliche Bauleitung: Suter + Suter GmbH, Düsseldorf
und Klaus Wolff in HWP Planungsgesellschaft mbH, Stuttgart
Freianlagen: Gerhart Teutsch + Partner, München
mit Volker Püschel, Mettmann (Örtliche Bauleitung)

Fachingenieure
Tragwerksplanung: Seeberger Friedl und Partner, München
Haustechnik-Planung: Biskamp und Partner, Bochum
mit Wiegand + Partner, Essen
Bauphysik: Richard Grün Institut, Ratingen
Vermessung: Ralf Arnscheidt, Essen

Daten
Planungsauftrag: Dezember 1993
Abbruch: März – Mai 1995
Baubeginn: Juni 1995
Fertigstellung: Juli 1997

Bruttogeschoßfläche: 26.126 m^2
Hauptnutzfläche: 9.363 m^2
Nebennutzfläche: 3.109 m^2
Umbauter Raum: 94.600 m^3
Gesamtprojektkosten: 76.000.000 DM